A Comprehensive Guide to Effective Dog Training Through
Positive Reinforcement

Kristin's Meet Me with Pawsitivity

"Successful dog training is built with patience, consistency and love."

Kristin Leest

"The Poodle Crew"

Four of our seven crew members

(Riley, Ruby, Ginger & Heidi)

Kristin's Meet Me with Pawsitivity:

A Comprehensive Guide to Effective Dog Training Through
Positive Reinforcement

Kristin Leest

DEDICATION

Because this book celebrates two of my greatest loves in the world – dogs and the art of dog training – I am delighted to dedicate it to my remarkable standard poodle companions: Hedi, Riley, Roxy, Ruby, Ginger, Hank, and Nala. Witnessing their journey from playful puppies to mature adults, with Heidi now being nine years old and holding the title of senior, fills my heart with gratitude and appreciation for the countless blessings they've brought to my family. These extraordinary dogs have not only enriched my life but have also left an indelible mark on my husband and our four children, Ryan, Maggie, Walter, and Patrick, as well as the numerous lovely puppies we've nurtured over the years.

Heidi, Riley, Roxy, Ruby, Ginger, Hank, and Nala have opened the door to my deepest passion: a profound love for canines. Whether it's through play, affection, or training, my mission has become finding ways to help them lead their most fulfilling lives. Along the way, I've accumulated knowledge and experiences, which I'm eager to share with you. I hope to impart the invaluable wisdom these wonderful companions have bestowed upon me, so that your furry friend can also experience their best life.

CONTENTS

Appendices

ACKNOWLEDGEMENTS

Embarking on the journey of writing a book has proven to be more challenging than I initially anticipated, yet the rewards surpass my wildest imagination. None of this would have been achievable without the unwavering support of my husband, Martin, who stands as one of my foremost advocates. Whether it was reviewing early drafts, providing technical assistance, or managing our children and pets to afford me the time to edit, his contribution to completing this book is as vital as my own.

I extend my deepest gratitude to my mother, Kathy, who has been my steadfast anchor throughout my life. Her support and insights into layout and creative design have been invaluable, and I am truly blessed to call her my mother.

A heartfelt acknowledgment goes to my sister, Amanda, my other rock, whose wisdom, words, and support played a crucial role in bringing this book to fruition. The bond between us, forged through overcoming challenges together, is a testament to an unparalleled sisterly friendship that I deeply cherish.

I express sincere thanks to Mahmuddidar, a remarkable resource and talented artist responsible for creating and designing the book cover. Your experience, knowledge, and insights brought the perfect creative touch to the project.

My heartfelt appreciation goes to my children—Ryan, Maggie, Walter, and Patrick—who have been integral to my journey. Your daily inspiration and presence have played a crucial role in my self-discovery. I am grateful to share and experience each moment with all of you.

Lastly, my gratitude extends to those instrumental in my journey, namely Jeff Smith, and Maria Batista. Each of you have left a profound impact on my life, making this entire endeavor possible. I am genuinely and humbly thankful for both of you.

LIST OF ILLUSTRATIONS

Welcome to the world of positive reinforcement dog training, where the transformative power of kindness and understanding unlocks the potential for a harmonious and fulfilling relationship with our four-legged companions. In the pages that follow, you will embark on a journey that explores the profound impact of positivity and reward-based methods in shaping your dog's behavior, fostering trust, and strengthening the bond between you and your furry friend.

Dog training has come a long way, and today, there is a growing recognition that harsh, punitive techniques are not only unnecessary but also harmful. Positive reinforcement, on the other hand, is built upon a foundation of empathy, science, and respect for the unique individuality of every dog. It's a philosophy that embodies compassion and the belief that good behavior is best achieved through rewards and positive experiences.

As you delve into this book, you'll discover the underlying principles of positive reinforcement and its practical applications in everyday dog training scenarios. You'll learn how to encourage desired behaviors, address unwanted habits, and navigate common challenges with a focus on encouragement rather than punishment. Whether you have a new puppy eager to learn, an older dog with established habits, or any canine companion in between, you'll find invaluable insights and techniques to guide you along the way.

Positive reinforcement is not only effective in achieving your training goals, but it also nurtures trust and a sense of security in your dog. By reinforcing the behaviors you desire, you create a happier and more confident pet. This method is not about bribery but about teaching your dog to make the right choices because they understand the benefits that come with them.

This approach empowers your dog to be an active participant in their own learning process.

Moreover, positive reinforcement training is an ongoing dialogue between you and your dog, a language of communication based on trust, cooperation, and shared experiences. It fosters a deep connection that goes beyond commands and obedience, to a relationship built on mutual understanding and shared joy.

In this book, you'll find a comprehensive guide to positive reinforcement training, packed with practical tips, real-life examples, and expert advice from experienced trainers. You'll be introduced to a world where patience, consistency, and the power of positive reinforcement can transform your dog into a well-behaved, happy, and eager-to-please companion.

So, I invite you to embrace this journey of discovery and enlightenment. The pages ahead are your roadmap to a more profound connection with your dog, one that is built on trust, respect, and the joy of shared learning. Through the principles and practices of positive reinforcement, you'll unlock the full potential of your furry friend and embark on a journey of companionship and understanding that will enrich both your lives.

Let this book be your guide, your source of inspiration, and your key to a world where you and your dog thrive together through kindness, encouragement, and positive reinforcement.

Happy reading and, more importantly, happy training!

Kristin

INTRODUCTION

Get ready for an extraordinary journey into the world of dog training, a world brimming with excitement and pawsitivity. In "Kristin's Meet Me with Pawsitivity: A Comprehensive Guide to Effective Dog Training through Positive Reinforcement," I'll be your guide on this exhilarating adventure.

Hi, I'm Kristin Leest, and I can't wait to share this fantastic journey with you. It's a world where we get to experience the quirkiest, funniest, most affectionate fur babies on the planet – our beloved dogs.

Here's a little something about me: I wear many hats. I'm a dog trainer, a wife, a mother of four, an American Kennel Club standard poodle breeder, a canine nutritional supplement creator, and a philanthropist. My journey with dogs began the moment I could walk and talk, but I've been training them professionally for the past fourteen years. In the last six years, my focus shifted to breeding and genetically health-testing Standard Poodles for families, support animals, and agility competition.

I share my life with an ever-growing poodle crew, who are family to us. In fact, while writing this book, our poodle crew of seven became eight when we welcomed Harry Winston, the son of Ruby and Hank, to our family. You'll see his charming photo in the last chapter, and you can find more snapshots of him on our Simply Standard Poodles website or my various social media platforms. I'm incredibly proud of him!

Why am I sharing all this with you? Because I believe you are the ideal reader for this book – someone like me, a passionate dog lover who's ready to give back and improve the lives of their canine companions. Like me, you're someone who works tirelessly to provide the best for their dogs, from nutrition to training, from wellness to socialization.

I understand the challenges you face because I face them too. I'm a hardworking mother of four, married to Martin, who just retired from the navy after twenty-one years. When I'm not writing, I'm immersing myself in canine health and wellness, training puppies and older dogs, managing multiple businesses, running a non-profit, and juggling the hectic schedules of four teenagers. We're your average, hardworking family, but what sets us apart is our deep love for our poodles. They've brought endless joy into our lives, and yes, they've even earned a spot in our bed.

So, who's the ideal reader? It's someone who, like us, is ready to make positive changes for their dogs. You might be excited, or perhaps a little unsure about where to begin. Either way, you're here because you want to make a difference for your furry companion. That's me too!

Over the past fourteen years, I've accumulated a wealth of knowledge and experience in dog training, psychology, health, and wellness. I've witnessed every stage of a dog's life, from birth to old age, and learned from veterinarians and certified dog trainers. Now, I feel compelled to share this wealth of knowledge with you because there's so much to explore, and the world of dog training is constantly evolving.

So, how do I manage my poodle crew and provide the best care for them? I do it the right way, every time. I don't cut corners because I've learned where it's crucial to invest in my dogs' health and well-being. Training is at the heart of that, and it's why I'm writing this book – to guide you on your journey to wellness with pawsitivity.

In the pages that follow, you'll discover how to train your dog using effective techniques and tools, all rooted in positive reinforcement. While some situations may require a certified trainer or behaviorist, I'll equip you with the knowledge to recognize when that's necessary.

We'll explore step-by-step guides for teaching your pup exciting new tricks, suitable for puppies as young as seven weeks old. You'll gain insights into understanding canine communication, the importance of socialization, and practical tips for house training, behavioral challenges, behavior modification plans, loose leash walking, off-leash walking, and recall techniques.

Advanced commands and tricks, harmonious multi-dog households, and success stories from fellow dog lovers will also be part of our journey. And at the end, you'll find tools to help you in your training efforts.

So, let's begin your wellness journey with pawsitivity. I can't wait to hear your success stories and witness your pup barking with confidence. Enjoy the adventure!

Heidi, Kristin's oldest poodle in the crew.

CHAPTER ONE

Successful Dog Training with Positive Reinforcement

Positive reinforcement within dog training involves offering an immediate reward, typically in the form of treats, praise, or play, following a desired behavior. This technique is designed to enhance the likelihood of the dog repeating the same behavior in the future (Hiby et al., 2004). Rooted in operant conditioning, positive reinforcement training aims to strengthen positive behaviors rather than relying on aversive methods that employ punishment to deter undesirable actions. Over time, this approach has gained widespread popularity due to its numerous advantages. It greatly enhances a dog's ability to learn and retain desired behaviors, as dogs learn through a process of trial and error. When they receive rewards for exhibiting desired actions, they are more inclined to repeat these behaviors, solidifying their understanding of expectations and promoting engagement in appropriate conduct (Yin, 2015).

Furthermore, this training method fosters a deep bond between dogs and their owners, as it revolves around rewarding desired behaviors with something the dog values or enjoys (Pryor, 1999). By prioritizing the encouragement of positive conduct over punishment for undesirable behavior, this method cultivates a constructive and cooperative learning environment (Blackwell et al., 2008). This trust forms the foundation of a positive and harmonious relationship, facilitating effective communication and understanding between humans and dogs.

Positive reinforcement training offers another notable advantage by effectively reducing fear and aggression in dogs. This positive approach avoids punitive measures, which, in turn, minimizes the likelihood of dogs experiencing stress, anxiety, or fear during their training (Blackwell et al., 2008). By sidestepping punitive techniques, positive reinforcement training serves as a preventive measure against unwanted behaviors and aggression, thus establishing a safer environment for both the dog and its human companions.

Moreover, positive reinforcement training finds its foundation in the neurobiology of reward systems. When a dog receives a reward for exhibiting a desired behavior, it triggers the release of dopamine in their brain, eliciting feelings of pleasure and satisfaction (Arhant et al., 2010). Furthermore, this approach has the potential to stimulate the release of oxytocin, a hormone associated with bonding and social connection (Mendl et al., 2010). These intricate neurobiological mechanisms actively contribute to the emotional well-being of dogs trained through positive reinforcement methods.

Positive reinforcement training also significantly contributes to a dog's emotional well-being. Dogs that undergo positive reinforcement training are notably less prone to experiencing anxiety, fear, or stress during their training sessions (Horowitz, 2009). As a result, they establish positive associations with their training experiences, cultivating a profound sense of happiness and contentment.

Furthermore, ethical considerations in dog training are intricately linked to the selection of training methods. Positive reinforcement training aligns seamlessly with ethical principles, placing a strong emphasis on the well-being and humane treatment of dogs. One of the primary ethical concerns in dog training revolves around the welfare of the animals involved, and positive reinforcement training places a paramount focus on preventing any pain or distress in dogs (Hiby et al., 2004). This ethical approach underscores the importance of prioritizing the emotional and physical well-being of our canine companions throughout the training process.

Key Principles of Positive Reinforcement Training

Dogs learn through the association of actions and consequences, a process known as reward-based learning. Rewards, such as treats, praise, toys, or play, strengthen the likelihood of a behavior recurring (Friedman, 2010). Timing is crucial in positive reinforcement training, as rewards should be given immediately after the desired behavior to reinforce the connection (Overall, 2013). Inconsistent or delayed rewards can cause confusion in your dog and lead to inconsistent results.

Positive reinforcement also relies on clear communication between you and your dog. Consistent cues and rewards help dogs understand what is expected of them (Horowitz, 2009). To keep your dog motivated, vary the rewards they receive for different tasks, taking into account each dog's specific preferences. This approach ensures successful training tailored to your dog's individual needs.

Benefits of Positive Reinforcement Training

Positive reinforcement training offers a multitude of benefits for both you and your canine companion, including improved communication, heightened confidence, and better behavior. This approach strengthens the bond between you and your dog, deepening your mutual understanding, as noted by Gazzano et al. (2010). Dogs trained with positive reinforcement often exhibit increased confidence and self-assuredness, as emphasized by McConnell (2002), resulting in enhanced behavior and obedience. The consistent rewards for desired behaviors have been proven to yield well-behaved and obedient dogs, as demonstrated by Herron et al. (2009). Furthermore, training sessions are enjoyable for dogs and can alleviate overall stress and anxiety, particularly in dogs with excess energy, as suggested by Landsberg et al. (2013).

The Psychology behind Positive Reinforcement

The psychology behind positive reinforcement is rooted in the work of B.F. Skinner, specifically operant conditioning. This theory explains how dogs learn to associate their actions or operant behavior with consequences. Positive reinforcement reinforces a desired behavior with an immediate reward, increasing the likelihood of its recurrence. Dogs actively engage in this voluntary learning process, making it a cooperative effort that enhances the effectiveness of positive reinforcement.

Practical Applications of Positive Reinforcement

Positive reinforcement can be applied to various aspects of dog training, including basic obedience training, crate training, housebreaking, socialization, and behavior modification. Positive reinforcement can be particularly effective in teaching commands like sit, stay, come, and place, as well as crate training and housebreaking. Socialization is crucial for a dog's health and well-being, and positive reinforcement can help create positive associations with new people, animals, and environments. For behavior modification, positive reinforcement can reduce aggression by reinforcing non-aggressive reactions in confrontational scenarios.

Significance of Positive Reinforcement

Positive reinforcement has been extensively researched and analyzed for over 80 years, making significant contributions to the field of behaviorism. It has been instrumental in understanding animal behavior and has shown that it can be one of the most powerful tools for shaping and changing a dog's behavior. Positive reinforcement fosters trust between dogs and their owners, reduces stress, and promotes lifelong learning. While it may not be the sole solution for all behavior issues, it is a versatile and adaptable training method that can be combined with other techniques for more complex cases.

The Techniques of Positive Reinforcement Training

Positive reinforcement training encompasses various techniques and exercises that can instill good behavior in your dog. Clicker training, luring and shaping, and targeting are some of the effective techniques you can employ to reinforce desired behaviors in your dog.

Troubleshooting with Positive Reinforcement Training

Challenges may arise in positive reinforcement training, such as when your dog is not motivated by treats, loses interest, or becomes distracted. To address these challenges, it's important to provide consistent rewards, offer breaks when needed, and gradually increase distractions during training. If your food-motivated dog loses interest in treats, consider alternative motivators based on your dog's breed and preferences.

Incorporating positive reinforcement into your dog's training regimen is a rewarding endeavor that not only shapes their behavior but also deepens the bond you share. In the next chapter, we will explore the significance of understanding your canine companion, delving into the intricacies of canine communication and behavior.

Ginger at 8 weeks old and a member of Kristin's poodle crew.

CHAPTER TWO

Setting the Foundation: Success in Training

In this chapter, we will explore the crucial steps to setting the foundation of a successful dog training experience. Preparing yourself for training, creating a positive training environment, and selecting the appropriate training tools are fundamental aspects of nurturing a well-behaved canine companion.

Preparing Yourself for Training

Effective dog training requires more than just teaching commands; it demands a comprehensive understanding of the training process, a willingness to adapt, and a realistic perspective on what can be achieved. As a dog trainer, your role extends beyond instructing your canine companion; it encompasses building a strong foundation, fostering effective communication, and managing your expectations. Before embarking on a training journey with your dog, it's essential to prepare yourself mentally and emotionally. Your mindset and approach play a significant role in the success of training.

Understanding Your Role as a Trainer

As a trainer, you play a vital role in the success of your dog. Taking the time to educate yourself about positive reinforcement techniques and the specific needs of your dog's breed or mix is necessary to your success (Overall, 2013). Knowledge is a powerful tool in training. The best trainers in the industry are the ones that come in with a tremendous amount of patience, a positive attitude, and create consistency throughout their program. Training takes time and requires consistent effort. You must be prepared for gradual progress and setbacks along the way (Horowitz, 2009).

Dogs can sense your emotions, so stay patient, calm, and encouraging (McConnell, 2002). Remain positive during training sessions even when it may or may not be going the way you wanted that specific day. As a dog trainer, your primary role is that of a teacher and communicator. You are responsible for conveying information, demonstrating desired behaviors, and providing clear cues to your dog. Effective communication forms the basis of successful training (Horowitz, 2009).

Your role also involves facilitating your dog's learning process. You must create an environment that encourages your dog to engage, think, and make choices. This promotes active learning and empowers your dog to be an active participant in the training (Donaldson, 1999).

Training is a lifelong journey. You are learning and growing every day, and it requires you and your dog to apply yourselves and try new ways to get something done if it doesn't seem to be sinking in. Your job as a trainer is to provide feedback to your dog, and reinforcement are essential components of dog training. You must offer timely and appropriate feedback to guide your dog's behavior. Positive reinforcement, such as treats, praise, or play, helps strengthen desired behaviors and encourages compliance (Reid, 1996).

Preparing Yourself for Dog Training

Before embarking on dog training, it's vital to educate yourself about canine behavior, learning theory, and various training techniques. Consider attending classes or seeking guidance from experienced trainers or behaviorists. This knowledge equips you to make informed decisions and employ effective training strategies (Serpell, 1996).

It will be important for you to set realistic goals for yourself as you begin your journey for dog training. As we mentioned earlier, training requires patience and consistency. Understand that dogs may not grasp concepts immediately, and behaviors can take time to develop. Consistency in your cues, rewards, and expectations is crucial for clarity and successful learning (McConnell, 2002).

Recognize that each dog is unique. Tailor your training approach to your dog's personality, age, and breed traits (Donaldson, 2008). Empathy towards your dog's perspective is essential. Recognize their individual temperament, preferences, and limitations. This empathetic approach fosters trust and cooperation (Pryor, 1984).

Lastly, be prepared to invest time in training. Short, consistent sessions are often more effective than long, sporadic ones for your dog (Blackwell et al., 2008). Dogs do better with shorter sessions. If you plan out what you want them to learn and you do it consistently every day, you will see better results than if you were to do once-a-week hour-long sessions with your dog.

Setting Realistic Expectations

It is important to set realistic expectations for you and your dog. Progress can vary depending on many variables of your pet, including age and personality. Dog training is a lifelong journey. It is like learning for humans. We learn and grow every day, and we should be doing that with dog training. There are going to be times when your dog just doesn't want to learn or practice that day. There are going to be times when a simple trick or what you may perceive as simple is difficult for your dog to grasp. It is okay. We all learn at different paces. Take a break and come back to it. Try a different tactic or skill. Don't give up. You got this! Here are some things to take into consideration when setting expectations.

Consider Gradual Progression

Realistic expectations involve recognizing that training is a gradual process. Dogs may not achieve perfection immediately, and progress may vary depending on the complexity of the behavior and the dog's previous experience. Take your time; repetition is key here. Consistency is key. Once you master one skill, move on to the next. Don't try to complete too many skills at once if it is overwhelming you and your dog.

Age and Breed Considerations

Acknowledge that age and breed can influence the speed and ease of training is very important. Puppies may require more patience and repetition, while some breeds are predisposed to excel in specific tasks. Do some research on the specific breed of your dog? Find out what motivates your dog. Is it food? Or is it toys? Is it play? Use these things to your advantage when you are training.

Recognize Individual Differences

Every dog is unique, with their own strengths, weaknesses, and quirks. Expecting uniform progress from all dogs disregards these individual differences. Tailor your training approach to your dog's specific needs (Freedman et al., 1961). By doing this, you will find you become a more effective trainer, and your dog is happier too. When you take the time to know and understand what drives your dog, it will help you to understand what motivates them to please you. Maybe they will do something because they want the praise. Or maybe it's for food or a toy. Take the extra time to really get to know your dog, and then train to their strengths. If they love chasing things, consider training for the fast CAT with the AKC. There are so many wonderful things you can do just by taking the time to really better understand your pets own individuality.

Challenges and Setbacks

Realistic expectations encompass the acknowledgment that challenges and setbacks are part of the training journey. Dogs may regress or struggle with certain behaviors, and it's essential to adapt your training methods accordingly. This can be frustrating for many. Maybe you took a break for a week, came back, and now your dog just can't do what they did last week. Or maybe they don't want to anymore. These things happen. Figuring out how to reestablish their motivation and get them excited about their time with you will be key. Going back to uncovering what motivates them will be helpful here in turning this around for you.

Creating a Positive Training Environment

Creating a positive training environment is crucial for your dog's success and overall well-being. This environment should be conducive to learning and free from distractions. This not only helps you focus but helps your dog focus too. You want your dog to associate a positive experience with one-on-one training and time with you. Doing this gives you the foundation to great success.

Location, Location, Location

Dogs have consistently demonstrated their preference for and thrive under consistent routines. Establishing a regular training schedule with consistent routines and training sessions conducted in the same location is instrumental in reinforcing learning, as emphasized by Overall (2013). When choosing a training location, it's essential to opt for a place that is both readily accessible for consistent visits and characterized by a calm atmosphere with minimal distractions. This conducive environment promotes your dog's focus during training and enhances information retention, in line with the insights shared by Landsberg et al. (2013). While the training location can be either indoors or outdoors, it's advisable to ensure that an outdoor setting is securely fenced for safety.

Tools and Training Aids for Success

Training aids for a positive training environment for dogs play a crucial role in facilitating effective training, fostering desired behaviors, and enhancing the learning experience for both dogs and their owners. These aids encompass a wide range of tools, devices, and equipment designed to assist trainers in teaching commands, addressing behavior issues, and ensuring the safety and well-being of their canine companions.

Here's a list of tools and training aids commonly used in positive dog training:

Treats and Food Rewards: High-value treats and small food rewards are essential for positive reinforcement. Use them to reward your dog for desired behaviors.

Clicker: A clicker is a small device that makes a distinct clicking sound. It's used to mark the exact moment your dog performs a desired behavior, signaling to your dog that a reward is coming.

Training Pouch: A training pouch or treat bag allows you to carry treats conveniently during training sessions. It keeps treats easily accessible and your hands free.

Leash and Collar/Harness: Choose a comfortable, well-fitting collar or harness and a sturdy leash for controlled training sessions, especially during leash walking and recall training.

Long Line: A long training leash (15-30 feet) gives your dog more freedom to move during training while maintaining control and safety.

Training Click Stick: This tool combines a clicker and a retractable target stick, making it useful for shaping behaviors and luring exercises.

Target Stick: A target stick is a handheld wand with a target at the end. It's used to guide your dog into specific positions or movements.

Mats and Targets: Use mats or targets to teach your dog specific positions, such as a "place" command or targeting exercises.

Interactive Toys and Puzzle Feeders: These toys provide mental stimulation and can be used to reward your dog during training. They are especially useful for dogs with high energy or intelligence.

Training Treat Dispensers: These devices dispense treats at intervals or when a specific action is performed. They can be helpful for teaching your dog to stay engaged and focused.

Training Whistle: A dog training whistle emits a sound at a frequency dogs can hear but is often inaudible to humans. It can be used as a cue or to get your dog's attention.

Tug Toys and Interactive Toys: Tug toys and interactive toys are excellent for teaching games and building a strong bond with your dog.

Target Training Props: These can include platforms, cones, and hoops, which are used in various training exercises to teach your dog to move in specific ways.

Training Treat Dispensing Pouch: A pouch with a wide opening that allows you too quickly and easily access treats while training.

Scent Samples: If you're teaching scent work or tracking, you may need scent samples to introduce your dog to specific scents.

Muzzle: In some cases, a muzzle may be necessary for safety during training, especially for dogs with a history of aggression or reactivity.

Video Camera: Recording training sessions can help you analyze your training techniques and track your dog's progress.

Notebook and Pen: Keeping a training journal helps you record your dog's achievements, challenges, and training goals.

Positive Reinforcement Books and Resources: Invest in books, online courses, and resources from experienced trainers to enhance your knowledge of positive reinforcement techniques.

Training Targets and Boundary Flags: Used to create visual cues and boundaries for your dog during training, especially for obedience and agility exercises.

Remember that while these tools and training aids are valuable, they should always be used in conjunction with positive reinforcement techniques and with the welfare of your dog in mind. Consult with a certified positive reinforcement trainer for guidance on selecting and using these tools effectively.

Understanding the Role of Training Aids

Understanding the role of training aids and how they serve as a valuable resource that complement the training process will be important to you as you begin your training journey. They assist trainers in conveying information, reinforcing behaviors, and ensuring the safety of dogs during training sessions. These aids can be categorized into several groups based on their functions and applications.

Benefits of Training Aids

The use of training aids provides numerous benefits in canine training and education, including improved focus, versatility, safety, enhanced communication, efficiency, and precision. Effective communication is a cornerstone of successful training, and training aids significantly enhance this aspect, leading to improved efficiency and precision.

As noted by Overall (2013), tools such as clickers and whistles offer clear and consistent cues to dogs, facilitating better understanding and faster learning. Additionally, treat pouches and target sticks, as suggested by Donaldson (1999), enhance training precision by enabling trainers to deliver rewards and cues with precision when needed. The ability to reward within seconds and employ tools like target sticks simplifies the training process, reduces confusion, and increases retention for your canine companion.

In some cases, additional tools like muzzles and anti-bark collars can ensure the safety of both dogs and trainers during training sessions, particularly when working with aggressive or vocal dogs. These aids offer an alternative approach if other training methods are ineffective. It's important to remember that each training aid serves a unique purpose and can support trainers in various aspects of training and developing a dog's abilities.

Agility equipment, as mentioned by Hiby et al. (2004), is another valuable training aid that helps dogs improve their focus, responsiveness, and physical fitness. Engaging in agility activities provides a fun and active way for dogs to exercise. There is a wide range of agility equipment available, including dog agility teeters, training dog walks, weave poles, tire jump panels, and more. If your dog enjoys agility activities, they may be eligible to compete in agility events with organizations like the AKC (American Kennel Club).

To participate in AKC agility competitions, dogs must be fifteen months of age or older, registered with the American Kennel Club, or listed with the AKC Indefinite Listing Privilege (ILP) program, which allows unregistered dogs of registerable breeds to compete in AKC Performance and Companion Events. While only purebred dogs can join the traditional AKC Purebred Registry or AKC Purebred Alternative Listing (PAL) programs, the AKC Canine Partners Program welcomes mixed and hybrid breed dogs of any age. This program allows dogs and their owners to enjoy and strengthen their bond through agility, as well as participate in various dog sports and earn titles. For more information on AKC Canine Partners and the American Kennel Club, you can visit their website at akc.org.

Reid (1996) highlights the importance of understanding that various types of training aids offer their own unique benefits, and it's essential to recognize that these aids cater to a wide range of training needs. Some aids are designed for basic obedience training, while others are tailored to advanced sports and training skills. The key to creating a more effective training program is to utilize these aids and adapt them to different training scenarios.

While training aids can be highly beneficial, it is equally crucial to use them responsibly and ethically. The welfare and comfort of your dogs should always be the top priority in training. Trainers must possess knowledge of the appropriate use of each training aid and understand when it is suitable to employ a specific tool. This approach, as emphasized by Blackwell (2008), is essential to avoid causing additional stress or harm to the dog. Any other approach would be contrary to the goal of positive reinforcement training, which is to train with a focus on promoting the well-being of the dog.

On the subsequent page, you will find a comprehensive, step-by-step guide for choosing the appropriate training tools and equipment tailored to various behaviors and training objectives. Should you have any questions during your training journey, we strongly recommend seeking guidance from a certified trainer or behaviorist in your local area for further information and assistance.

Step-by-Step Guide:

How to Select the Right Training Tools & Equipment

Choosing the right training tool for your dog depends on several factors, including your dog's personality, specific training goals, and your personal preferences. Here are some steps to help you select the appropriate training tool:

Step 1: Identify Your Training Goals.

Determine what specific behaviors or commands you want to train your dog. Are you working on basic obedience, advanced tricks, or addressing behavioral issues? Your training goals will influence the choice of tools.

Step 2: Understand Your Dog's Personality.

Consider your dog's temperament and sensitivity. Some dogs respond well to positive reinforcement techniques, while others may require more structured training tools.

Step 3: Research and Consult.

Meet with experienced trainers or behaviorists for guidance on suitable training tools for your specific needs. They can provide valuable insights and recommendations.

Step 4: Utilize Positive Reinforcement.

Using techniques which often involve treats, praise, and toys. Positive reinforcement is a gentle and effective approach for most dogs.

Step 5: Start with basic tools.

Begin with only the essentials like a clicker, target stick, or treat pouch to focus on reinforcing good behavior. These tools can be used for a wide range of training purposes and are great for training the fundamentals.

Step 6: Use a leash and collar/harness.

Make sure to be using a leash and collar/harness in your training and that the one you choose fits comfortably on your dog. Avoid using a choke or prong collar, unless it is specifically recommended by a certified trainer or behaviorist for the specific goal you are looking to accomplish.

Step 7: Consider the leash length.

When using a leash for training, shorter leashes are useful for more control, while longer leads can provide more freedom during off-leash training.

Step 8: Consulting with a professional.

When tackling specific behavioral issues like aggression, separation anxiety, or leash reactivity, consult with a professional trainer who can recommend additional specialized tools or techniques.

Step 9: Gradually introduce a new tool.

Introduce new tools slowly and with positive associations and rewards. Make sure your dog is comfortable with the tool before incorporating it into your training.

Step 10: Evaluate your progress.

Continuously assess your dog's progress throughout their training, you may need to adjust your training tools. If you notice any adverse reactions or discomfort during a training session, consider alternative tools or methods.

Step 11: Safety is always first.

First and foremost during training, you want to ensure that the chosen training tool is safe for your dog. Avoid any tools that may cause harm or distress.

Positive Reinforcement Tools

Positive reinforcement tools are integral to effective dog training as they emphasize rewarding and reinforcing desired behaviors. These tools encompass treats, clicker training, and the inclusion of toys. Additionally, we'll delve into the significance of leashes and collars, the proper utilization of crates and confinement tools, and the selection of training aids to support your training endeavors and how to implement them effectively.

Leveling Up With Your Training Treats

Treats are a fundamental component in positive reinforcement training, providing immediate rewards for your dog's good behavior. These rewards can come in various forms, including dry kibble, soft treats, freeze-dried meats, or even homemade options. When selecting treats for your dog, it's essential to choose ones that are highly motivating and appealing. The type of dog treat you use can significantly impact the success of your training sessions. The right training treat helps your dog focus, but it's crucial to strike a balance as overly enticing treats might distract from the training task. For instance, some trainers prefer using hot dogs or cut-up string cheese.

Given the plethora of treat options, you might wonder which dog treats to purchase. The answer is simple: use the training treats your dog enjoys. However, it's important to distinguish between high-value, medium-value, and low-value treats. Let's explore these differences and provide some recommendations for each.

High-value Treats

High-value treats are typically moist, freeze-dried, highly aromatic, and something your dog rarely receives outside of training sessions. Think of tiny pieces of chicken, liverwurst, tripe, or even a bit of peanut butter (make sure it's xylitol-free) smeared on a spoon. It's essential to avoid using high-fat foods, such as bacon or sausage, to prevent your dog from experiencing an upset stomach or potentially developing pancreatitis.

High-value treats should be used in specific training scenarios to maximize their effectiveness:

- When introducing a completely new behavior to your dog.

- In highly distracting environments, like a crowded group dog training class.

- As a reward for a quick and high-quality response to a cue or command.

- During essential socialization and proactive exposure training sessions for puppies.

- When working on counter conditioning as part of a behavior modification plan for issues like leash reactivity, aggression, anxiety, or fear.

Medium-value Treats

Medium value treats, as the name implies, fall between high-value and low-value treats. They are typically semi-moist or dry treats made from ingredients not found in your dog's regular food. These treats are given more frequently during training sessions and in everyday routines compared to high-value treats.

You should use medium value treats in the following scenarios:

- When reinforcing an already learned behavior.

- In mildly distracting environments.

- As rewards for good behavior throughout the day.

- As part of regular enrichment activities.

Low-value Treats

Low-value treats are perfect for integrating into your training regimen because they are lower in calories than high and medium value dog treats. These treats are usually dry and crunchy, and many trainers use their dog's regular food for this level of treating. Having a low-value treat option is essential for gradually reducing the use of treats in training.

Low-value treats should be used in the following situations:

- If your dog performs a requested cue, but it's a below average performance, this may indicate that your dog needs more distance from a distraction or a step back in their training.

- Throughout the day to encourage ongoing good behavior.

- In low to no distraction training environments.

- As part of regular enrichment activities.

- When you're working on phasing out the use of treats for a specific behavior.

It's important to determine which level each treat falls into for your dog. Observe their response and use this as your guide for incorporating treats into your training program. However, before doing so, be sure to check the treat ingredients to ensure they don't contain anything that your dog may be allergic or sensitive to.

When you're ready to use these treats in the training process, make sure to offer them immediately after your dog performs the desired behavior to establish a connection between the reward and the action. High-value treats are especially useful for complex or challenging tasks, while lower-value treats can be used for simpler commands. Be mindful of portion sizes to prevent overfeeding, and consider breaking treats into smaller pieces for frequent rewards. Some recommended treat options include dried beef lung, your dog's kibble, cut-up hot dogs, and string cheese.

Clicker Training

Clicker training is a method that uses a handheld device called a clicker to mark the exact moment when your dog exhibits a desired behavior. The clicker sound is followed by a reward (usually a treat). The clicker provides precise timing and consistency in marking the behavior you want to reinforce. It helps your dog understand which action led to the reward. Before using the clicker in training, you should click and reward your dog multiple times without any specific behavior first. This conditions your dog to associate the click with a reward. Then begin to train.

The Value of Dog Toys: Priceless

Toys play a vital role in a dog's overall health and well-being, serving as a necessity rather than a luxury. They offer several benefits, including combating boredom, providing comfort during moments of nervousness, preventing behavior problems, discouraging chewing on household items, and aiding dogs with separation anxiety. Additionally, they serve as a tool to reinforce positive behavior, especially for dogs highly motivated by play.

Having a variety of toys is important because dogs can become bored with the same ones. It's recommended to maintain a collection of toys, with pet owners rotating a couple of them each day to keep their dog engaged and entertained. This practice ensures that the dog doesn't grow tired of their toys.

Puppies, in particular, benefit from a wide assortment of toys since they are more energetic and have shorter attention spans, making them prone to boredom.

There are various types of toys, including chew toys, puzzle toys, and interactive toys, each with its unique benefits:

Chew Toys: These support dental health, provide anxiety relief, and are excellent for teething puppies. Chewing helps scrape away plaque and tartar buildup and helps dogs cope with anxiety and stress, reducing the likelihood of them chewing on furniture.

Puzzle Toys: These exercise a dog's mind and body, alleviate boredom, and are ideal for fast eaters. Pet owners can place treats or kibble inside puzzle toys, providing hours of entertainment and enhancing problem-solving skills.

Interactive Toys: These include puzzles, robotic games, and ball launchers, treat dispensers, tug-of-war toys, hide and seek toys, and more. They assist with diet management, boredom relief, behavior prevention, and anxiety reduction.

Choosing the right toys depends on your dog's preferences and energy level. Incorporating toys into a training session can make training more enjoyable. You can turn a toy into a training game by requiring your dog to perform commands like "sit" before you throw a ball or "leave it" before they can play with a toy. These strategies leverage your dog's motivation during training.

Remember that the effectiveness of a toy or tool depends on your dog's individual preferences. Some dogs are more food-motivated, while others are toy-driven or enjoy sounds like a clicker or squeaker. The key is to use the toy or tool that your dog finds most rewarding.

Furthermore, always ensure that when using toys in conjunction with positive reinforcement techniques, you accompany them with clear and consistent communication, patience, and a focus on rewarding the behaviors you want to reinforce. Positive reinforcement works best when used alongside training tools that prioritize rewards over punishment.

The Importance of Collars and Leashes

The effectiveness of any collar or harness depends on the individual dog and their specific training needs. Positive reinforcement training focuses on rewarding desired behaviors and creating a positive learning experience for the dog, so choosing equipment that minimizes discomfort and fear is essential. Consulting with a professional dog trainer can help you select the most suitable collar or harness for your dog and training goals is most important when deciding which to choose however we have provided a list of all the different options available to you as you begin your training. Remember it is important to choose collars that prioritize the dog's comfort and safety while still allowing for effective communication.

Flat Collar: These are traditional collars made from materials like nylon or leather. They are comfortable for everyday wear and can hold identification tags. They are suitable for positive reinforcement training when used to attach a leash for basic commands like sit, stay, and come.

Martingale Collar: Also known as a limited-slip collar, it provides more control over a dog without choking or harming them. It's often used for training dogs that tend to slip out of regular flat collars and are useful for dogs with slender necks.

Harness: A dog harness is designed to encircle the dog's body, evenly distributing pressure, unlike collars that rest around the neck. Front-clip harnesses, in particular, prove advantageous for training purposes as they discourage pulling and provide improved control. According to McConnell (2002), harnesses are often a superior option for dogs that tend to pull on the leash because they minimize strain on the neck and enhance control during walks.

Head Collar (Halti or Gentle Leader): These collars fit over the dog's muzzle and neck, giving the handler control of the dog's head movements. They can be useful for managing pulling and discouraging lunging.

Back-Clip Harness: These harnesses have the leash attachment on the back and can be suitable for dogs that are already well-behaved on a leash.

Front-Clip Harness: Harnesses with the leash attachment on the front can help prevent pulling and encourage dogs to walk politely on a leash.

Body Harness: These harnesses wrap around the dog's body and can provide more control over larger or stronger dogs. They are often used for positive reinforcement training.

Clicker Training Collar: This is not a traditional collar but rather a device that makes a clicking sound. It's used in combination with treats to mark and reinforce desired behaviors during training.

Training Collar (Choke Chain or Prong Collar): While these are not typically associated with positive reinforcement, some trainers use them cautiously with positive methods to address specific issues. However, it's important to seek professional guidance if considering these collars, as improper use can harm the dog.

When practicing positive reinforcement training with dogs, you have various leash options to choose from to ensure your dog's comfort and safety. Here is a list of different styles of leashes that are commonly used during dog training exercises in parallel with positive reinforcement techniques:

Standard Leash: A traditional leash made of materials like nylon or leather. It provides a basic level of control and is suitable for basic obedience training.

Retractable Leash: These leashes have a spring-loaded mechanism that allows you to extend or retract the length of the leash. They can be useful for training recall (coming when called) and giving your dog more freedom while still maintaining control.

Long Line: A long line leash is typically made of nylon and can be 15-50 feet long. It provides your dog with more freedom while still being under control, making it great for practicing recalls and allowing your dog to explore safely.

Training Tab: A short, handle-like leash that's usually 6-12 inches in length. It's used for close control during training and can be attached to a regular leash or collar.

Hands-Free Leash: These leashes can be worn around your waist or over your shoulder, allowing you to keep your hands free while still maintaining control over your dog. They are great for activities like running or hiking.

Martingale Lead: A combination of a leash and a martingale collar, this type of lead can help gently control your dog's movements without causing discomfort or choking.

Slip Lead: A combination of a leash and a slip collar. It provides a quick and simple way to control your dog without needing a separate collar.

Bungee Leash: These leashes have a bungee or shock-absorbing section that helps reduce jolts and pulls, providing a more comfortable experience for both you and your dog.

Traffic Lead: A very short leash, usually 1-2 feet long, designed for use in crowded areas or when you need to keep your dog close by.

Multi-Function Leash: Some leashes come with multiple attachment points or handles, allowing you to adjust the length and configuration as needed for training purposes.

When selecting a leash for positive reinforcement training, it's important to consider your dog's size, behavior, and training goals. Additionally, choose a leash that is comfortable for both you and your dog, and always ensure that it is in good condition and securely attached to your dog's collar or harness to ensure safety during training sessions. Depending on what you are training and the age of the dog determines the type of collar and leash you would use. For example if you have a six month old dog learning basic obedience they may only be a fifteen pound cocker spaniel you may train with a martingale collar and leash combo. If you are training a one year old Belgian Malinois and you are training obedience and military tactical training and search training you might have three different collars on your dog so that you can go back and forth in style and lesson with your dog.

Effective Confinement Tools

Effective confinement tools play a crucial role in the realm of positive reinforcement dog training. They serve as invaluable assets, facilitating the creation of a secure and controlled environment that proves particularly beneficial when working on obedience or addressing specific canine issues. In the following discussion, we will explore several such effective confinement tools tailored for positive reinforcement training, commencing with the crate.

A crate is a small, enclosed space that acts as a secure and comfortable haven for your dog, accommodating various training purposes. Whether you are house training, preventing destructive behaviors, or instilling impulse control, the crate serves as a versatile tool. It is essential to ensure that the crate's dimensions allow your dog to stand, turn around, and lie down comfortably, promoting a sense of safety and security. The key to using the crate effectively lies in creating a positive association through positive reinforcement. When your dog willingly enters the crate, reward them with treats, toys, and praise. Gradually extend the duration your dog spends in the crate, ensuring they associate it with positive experiences while avoiding any punitive use of the crate.

Another valuable confinement tool is the exercise pen, an adjustable and portable enclosure that offers more expansive confinement than a crate. It is especially useful when you seek to grant your dog more space while maintaining control. These exercise pens are versatile and can be configured into various shapes and sizes. They serve as excellent tools for managing your dog's environment during training sessions, puppy-proofing a room, and providing a secure area for play. These enclosures prevent your dog from accessing potentially hazardous areas or items while permitting movement and play. Keep in mind that exercise pens come in varying heights, so be sure to research and select one that matches your dog's size and needs.

Baby gates are another effective tool, providing controlled access to specific areas within your home. They are particularly advantageous for containing puppies or dogs in designated training spaces. By utilizing baby gates, you can create a controlled environment conducive to working on obedience commands, house manners, and other training exercises. Gradual introduction of your dog to the baby gates, paired with positive reinforcement, rewards them for remaining within the designated area. Remember that the effectiveness of these gates may vary based on their height, with larger dogs potentially being able to leap over them.

Tethering, another confinement method, entails attaching your dog to a fixed point using a leash or a long line. This technique proves useful for teaching impulse control, encouraging calm behavior, and preventing unwanted actions. Tethering should always occur under supervision to ensure your dog's safety, and dogs should never be left tethered unattended. When using tethering as a training tool, be sure to reward your dog for maintaining a calm and well-behaved disposition while tethered, reinforcing positive behavior and promoting self-control.

Lastly, playpens and indoor fences offer another exceptional confinement approach, providing a larger enclosed space within your home that supports controlled play and training sessions. These tools are particularly advantageous for puppies and small dogs, permitting safe play and exploration while restricting access to restricted areas. These confinement options can serve as invaluable tools in a variety of training scenarios, with the fundamental principle being to reward your dog for displaying calm and desirable behavior within the confined space. It is imperative that the confinement area is comfortable, safe, and equipped with access to water and appropriate toys to engage your dog both mentally and physically. Confinement should always be approached as a constructive and positive training tool rather than a form of punishment.

Effective Training Aids

Effective training aids are essential tools in positive reinforcement training for dogs. These aids help trainers and pet owners reinforce desired behaviors, communicate effectively with their dogs, and create a positive learning environment. Treats and food rewards are one of the most versatile and effective training aids for dogs. They serve as immediate rewards for desired behaviors and motivate dogs to repeat those behaviors. Use can use a variety of treat types, including small, soft treats, freeze-dried meats, or even your dog's regular kibble, depending on your dog's preferences. Offer treats immediately after your dog performs the desired behavior to reinforce the association between the action and the reward. For more challenging tasks use more high-value treats and lower-value treats for simpler commands.

Clicker or Marker Training is another effective training aid. Clicker training uses a handheld clicker (or another distinct sound, like a verbal marker) to mark the exact moment your dog exhibits the desired behavior. The sound is followed by a reward (usually a treat). Clicker training provides precise timing and consistency, helping your dog understand which action led to the reward. Before using the clicker in training, you should click it and treat your dog multiple times without any specific behavior. This conditions your dog to associate the click with a reward.

Target Sticks and Target Training is another great aid. Target sticks are long, thin devices that dogs can touch with their noses or paws. They are used in target training to teach dogs specific behaviors or positions by guiding them with the stick. For example, you can use a target stick to guide your dog into a "sit" or "down" position, making it easier for them to understand the desired posture.

A training harness or a specialized training harness, like a no-pull harnesses or front-clip harness for example, is a great training aid that can provide excellent control during walks that is effective at discouraging pulling. There are also No-Pull Harnesses which can be used to redirect your dog's forward motion when they pull, making it more comfortable for them to walk by your side.

A valuable training tool is the Long Line or Lead, which typically ranges from 10 to 30 feet in length, offering controlled freedom during training sessions. According to Landsberg et al. (2013), using a leash extension can grant your dog more liberty during outdoor training while maintaining your ability to exert control. Long lines are especially beneficial for training recall and off-leash obedience in secure environments. It's essential to employ long lines in safe settings to prevent your dog from wandering off while still permitting them to explore and practice commands. For instance, when working on the "come" command, a long lead can be employed to maintain control while allowing the dog more flexibility to move away from your side over greater distances. If necessary, you can gently guide or correct the dog to return when called by reeling in the lead. In summary, when training the "come" command, a long lead empowers you to balance control and your dog's freedom of movement, providing an effective way to reinforce recall training.

Puzzle Toys and Interactive Feeders can be fun and engaging aids for your dog mentally and physically. Just fifteen minutes with a puzzle toy is equal to thirty minutes of exercise outside. It can be a great tool for rainy days to curb boredom and build enrichment. These toys encourage problem-solving and can help teach patience and impulse control.

Target Mats are effective when used as designated "place" areas teaching your dog to go to a specific spot and stay there until released. (Great tool for assisting in learning the "place" command.) Place training is especially useful for teaching your dog to settle calmly during meal times, when guests arrive and you need to answer the front door, or when you need them to stay in one area for a short period of time.

Whistle Commands are often used when giving commands or signals at a distance, particularly in outdoor settings, where vocal commands may not carry as effectively. Your dog should be conditioned to understand specific whistle commands and associate them with positive reinforcement.

When employing positive reinforcement techniques alongside these training tools, trainers can effectively attain their desired outcomes to the fullest extent. In the course of training, it's crucial to consistently reward your dog generously for the desired behavior, exercise patience, and maintain unwavering consistency throughout the entire training session. Your selection of training aids should take into account your dog's individual preferences and training objectives, so be sure to assess what suits your dog's needs best and make adjustments as required.

How to Clicker Train Your Dog

Clicker training is a positive reinforcement technique used for training dogs, relying on a bridging stimulus, the clicker, within the framework of operant conditioning. This approach employs conditioned re-enforcer's, allowing trainers to provide quicker and more precise feedback compared to primary re-enforcers like food. The effectiveness of clicker training is enhanced when it's integrated with positive reinforcement methods because the distinctive clicking sound is more discernible for your dog and can be delivered more rapidly than verbal commands.

A Step-by-Step Guide:

How to Clicker Train Your Dog

Acquire the Necessary Supplies:

- A clicker
- Martingale collar
- Leash
- Treats (small, soft, and highly motivating),
- Treat pouch to hold your treats
- Dog waste bags in case of accidents at the training site

Using the Clicker:

Step 1: Begin in a quiet area with your dog.
Hold the clicker in one hand and a treat in the other.

Step 2: Click the clicker.
Immediately give your dog a treat. Repeat this process several times in quick succession.

Step 3: Observe your dog's response.
The goal is for your dog to associate the sound of the clicker with receiving a reward.

Step 4: Pick a behavior your dog does naturally.
Start with a simple or basic behavior that your dog is familiar with, such as "sit" or "come."

Step 5: Wait for your dog to naturally offer the behavior.
As soon as your dog performs the desired behavior, immediately click the clicker and reward with a treat.

Ex. If your dog sits on their own, click and treat.

Step 6: Practice this multiple times in short training sessions.
Be consistent with your clicks and rewards. Keep training session's brief, especially if your dog is new to clicker training.

Step 7: Pair the verbal cue with the click and treat.
Once your dog is consistently responding to the clicker, introduce verbal cues. For example, say "sit" just before you expect your dog to perform the behavior. Over time, your dog will learn to associate the cue with the behavior.

Step 8: For complex tricks, reward small steps first.
Break the behavior down into small steps and reward small behavior successes until they master the main desired behavior. As your dog becomes more skilled, you can start shaping more complex behaviors.

Ex. If you're teaching "roll over," you might initially reward your dog for lying on their side, then for rolling partway, and finally for completing the full roll.

Step 9: Be consistent with your clicker and treat timing.
Click the moment your dog performs the behavior you want and follow up with an immediate reward.

Step 10: Be patient. Allow your dog to progress at their pace.
When you dog is proficient, gradually increase the difficulty of the behaviors you're training.

Step 11: Maintain a positive and enjoyable atmosphere.

Praise and celebrate your dog's successes during training, and avoid scolding or punishment.

Step 12: Continue consistent and frequent practice.

For your dog to retain and generalize their training you will need to practice consistently and frequently and in various environments with different distractions as they become more proficient.

Step 13: Keep track of your dog's progress.

Adjust your training goals as needed for your dog. Each dog's abilities are different. Be flexible and adapt the training to your dog's needs.

Remember that clicker training should always be a positive and rewarding experience for your dog. It helps to create a strong bond between you and your canine companion while promoting mental stimulation and a positive overall sense of well-being.

As you begin preparing yourself for training, setting up your positive training environment, and selecting the right training tools understand that you are establishing the foundation and building blocks of a successful training journey for you and your companion. With your commitment to understanding your role as a trainer, setting realistic expectations for you and your fur baby, and creating an environment that is conducive to canine learning you have just paved the way for a well-behaved and happy canine.

Training a dog can be a demanding endeavor, and to ensure your efforts are fruitful, you must possess patience, consistency, empathy, and a willingness to adapt to any challenges or setbacks that may arise. By adequately preparing for the training journey and establishing realistic expectations, you can initiate the process of forging a strong connection with your furry friend, ultimately achieving significant and enduring results. These training tools cater to a wide range of training needs, encompassing basic obedience, specialized sports, and behavior modification. When employed responsibly and ethically, these aids can significantly contribute to the cultivation of well-behaved, obedient, and content canine companions.

In the upcoming chapter, we will explore the profound realm of understanding your canine companion, delving into the intricacies of canine communication, behavior, and body language.

Nala & Ginger at Halloween, members of Kristin's poodle crew.

3

CHAPTER THREE

Understanding Canine Communication

Understanding the methods of communication employed by your canine companions, encompassing both verbal and non-verbal cues, is vital for establishing a harmonious relationship between the dog and the trainer, ultimately leading to genuinely effective training results. In this chapter, we will delve into the art of interpreting dog body language, the skill of listening to your dog, and the techniques for building trust and fostering a deeper connection.

Deciphering Canine Body Language

Dogs primarily communicate through their body language, and the skill to interpret these signals is indispensable for understanding their emotions and drives. Proficiency in reading and interpreting their body language equips a trainer with a valuable skill that frequently facilitates a deeper connection with the dog. Identifying signs of canine insecurity or frustration before others can enable a trainer to address and potentially resolve behavioral issues more promptly than their peers. Therefore, the more adept one becomes at comprehending the canine language, the more effective they can be as a trainer.

Key Elements of Canine Body Language

Key aspects of canine body language stem from their outward appearance and how they present themselves to the world. Begin by examining their body posture, as it can reveal much about their emotional state, as noted by Donaldson (2008). Are they standing upright and displaying confidence or crouched and appearing fearful?

Further observation should encompass their facial expressions and features, which include ear position, eye contact, and how they position their mouth or lips. Ears can be upright, relaxed, or pinned back, with erect ears indicating alertness and pinned-back ears signaling fear or submission, as explained by Overall

(2013). Direct eye contact can be interpreted as a challenge in the language of dogs, with a relaxed gaze indicating comfort and a hard stare potentially indicating tension, as suggested by McConnell (2002). A relaxed, slightly open mouth typically indicates comfort, while snarling or baring teeth can signify aggression or discomfort, according to Blackwell et al. (2008).

Additionally, the position and movement of the tail play a significant role in conveying a dog's emotions, including feelings of happiness, nervousness, fear, fright, or uncertainty. Hoeowitz (2009) notes that a wagging tail can express excitement or joy, while a tucked tail may reveal fear or submission. The entirety of a dog's outward body language provides valuable insights for tailoring your training approach to the specific needs of that dog at any given moment.

Stress Signals in Dogs

Just like humans, dogs can encounter stress in different circumstances. Identifying signs of stress in your dog is crucial for their overall well-being and enables you to address and alleviate the root causes of their anxiety. It's vital to be attuned to your dog's body language as stress can manifest in various ways. For instance, a nervous or anxious dog may exhibit behaviors like excessive lip licking, unusual yawning, or panting more than usual. Being able to recognize these stress indicators empowers you to adapt your training environment or methods effectively, as suggested by Landsberg et al. (2013).

Here are some common signs of stress in dogs:

Body Language

- **Tucked Tail:** A dog may tuck their tail between their legs, signaling discomfort or fear.

- **Piloerection:** When the fur on a dog's back stands up, it can indicate heightened arousal or stress.

- **Panting and Drooling:** Excessive panting and drooling, especially in non-hot conditions, can be a sign of stress.

Behavioral Changes

- **Aggression or Agitated Behavior**: Dogs may become more aggressive or reactive when stressed. They may growl, snap, or bark excessively.

- **Withdrawal:** Some dogs withdraw or become unusually quiet when stressed, avoiding interaction or hiding.

- **Excessive Barking or Whining:** Increased vocalization can be a sign of distress or anxiety.

- **Destructive Behavior**: Dogs may chew furniture, dig, or engage in other destructive behaviors when anxious.

Changes in Appetite

- **Loss of Appetite:** Stress can lead to a decreased interest in food or even refusal to eat.

- **Overeating**: In some cases, stress can cause a dog to overeat or engage in stress-induced binge eating.

Toileting Issues

- **Accidents:** House-trained dogs may have accidents indoors when stressed.

- **Inappropriate Urination or Defecation**: Stress can also lead to urinating or defecating in unusual places.

- **Excessive Licking or Scratching:** Dogs may engage in excessive grooming, licking, or scratching as a coping mechanism when stressed.

- **Restlessness:** Restless behavior, such as pacing or an inability to settle down, can indicate stress.

- **Changes in Body Posture:** A stressed dog may cower, slouch, or lower their body closer to the ground.

- **Excessive Yawning:** Regular yawning, particularly when not linked to fatigue, may indicate stress. According to Turid Rugaas (2005), yawning in dogs doesn't solely correlate with tiredness or boredom. Excessive yawning can signify stress, particularly in situations where the dog is not physically fatigued. Yawning can function as a calming signal, representing the dog's effort to relieve tension and communicate that it poses no threat.

- **Excessive Shedding:** Stress can lead to increased shedding in dogs.

- **Excessive Salivation**: Some dogs may drool excessively when stressed.

- **Vomiting or Diarrhea:** Stress can lead to gastrointestinal upset, resulting in vomiting or diarrhea.

- **Paw Lifting:** Dogs may lift one of their paws as if it's bothering them when stressed.

- **Lip smacking:** Lip smacking in dogs refers to the repetitive action of licking their lips or nose, often done slowly and deliberately. This behavior can arise as a reaction to anxiety, nervousness, or discomfort. It is classified as a displacement behavior, indicating that the dog is attempting to manage stress or internal conflict by channeling its energy into lip smacking, as explained by Overall (2013).

- **Excessive Panting:** While panting is a normal cooling mechanism for dogs, excessive panting, especially when not preceded by physical activity or heat, can be indicative of stress. It is a way for dogs to dissipate excess energy and regulate their body temperature during anxious moments.

It's important to note that individual dogs may exhibit stress differently, and some may show subtle signs that are easy to miss. Additionally, the context in which the behavior occurs is crucial for understanding whether it's due to stress or another issue. If you suspect your dog is stressed, consider the environment, recent changes, or triggers that may be causing their anxiety. If your dog is consistently displaying signs of stress, consult with a veterinarian or a professional dog behaviorist to determine the cause and develop a plan to help your dog manage their stress and anxiety effectively.

Tail Wagging Myths

Contrary to popular belief, a wagging tail does not always indicate a friendly dog. The speed, height, and context of the wag is crucial. According to Horowitz (2009) a stiff, high wag can indicate arousal or aggression, while a loose, low wag typically signals friendliness. Beyond tail types, the position and movement of a dog's tail is crucial in interpreting their communication.

The following are some common tail positions and their meanings:

- **High and Stiff Tail:** A high and stiff tail is typically held up-right, and the dog's body appears tense. This posture often indicates alertness, excitement, or even aggression. Breeds like the Samoyed exhibit this tail position when excited.

- **Low and Tucked Tail:** A low and tucked tail is held close to the body, indicating submission, fear, or anxiety. Dogs often display this tail position when feeling threatened or uncomfortable.

- **Wagging Tail:** A wagging tail is one of the most familiar tail movements. While wagging can indicate happiness and excitement, the speed, direction, and context of the wag matter. A fast, stiff wag may signal aggression or overstimulation, while a slow and loose wag typically reflects a relaxed and content mood.

- **Tail between the Legs:** A tail tucked between the legs is a clear sign of fear, submission, or anxiety. Dogs may display this posture when encountering unfamiliar or intimidating situations.

- **Curled Tail:** A curled tail can indicate playfulness or friendliness, especially when paired with other relaxed body language.

Dog tails serve as multifaceted communication tools, providing valuable cues regarding a dog's mood, emotions, and intentions.

A comprehensive grasp of the diverse types of dog tails, their positions, and movements empowers us to accurately decipher canine behavior. A wagging tail can express joy or excitement, while a tucked tail may signify fear or submission. Various tail types, including straight, curled, or sickle shapes, are distinct to specific breeds and offer insights into their lineage.

Demonstrating respect for and responding to a dog's tail language is pivotal in cultivating trust and fostering a strong bond between dogs and their human counterparts. It enables us to discern when a dog is at ease, anxious, thrilled, or requires personal space. Ultimately, the study of dog tails exemplifies the intricate ways in which dogs communicate with both us and their fellow canines, enriching our understanding of these cherished companions.

The Art of Listening to Your Dog

Effective dog training involves not only teaching commands but also understanding and responding to the dog's emotional state. Dogs communicate their feelings through body language, vocalizations, and other subtle cues. When a dog is stressed or anxious, it may exhibit behaviors like lip smacking, yawning, and excessive panting. Recognizing and interpreting these signals is crucial for modifying training methods and ensuring the dog's well-being.

According to McConnell, (2002) listening to your dog goes beyond just hearing their vocalizations, it involves observing their behavior, understanding their needs, and responding appropriately. This skill is vital for building a strong and mutually respectful bond.

Why It's Important to Listen to These Signals

In the realm of training and working with dogs, it is of paramount importance to heed your dog's stress signals, as they offer invaluable insights into your canine companion. By taking the time to comprehend these signals, you embark on the journey of establishing a robust foundation of trust between you and your dog. This trust is a pivotal factor in the success of your role as a trainer. Disregarding these signals can erode this essential trust.

It's crucial to recognize that stressed dogs often struggle with learning new behaviors and commands. Addressing their stress is the key to making training a more enjoyable and effective experience for both the dog and the trainer. Ideally, a dog should not undergo excessive stress during training. As a responsible trainer, your goal should be to minimize stress as much as possible.

Being able to identify stress signals enables the trainer to uphold the dog's well-being and mental health as a top priority, which is of utmost importance in achieving effective training outcomes. This is not only about welfare but also about safety. Stressed dogs can exhibit unpredictable or reactive behavior, potentially leading to unsafe situations during training sessions.

By emphasizing their welfare, creating a comfortable and conducive learning environment, and placing a strong focus on safety, you establish a winning trifecta for training success.

Modifying Training for Stressed Dogs

Modifying training for dogs experiencing stress is of utmost importance to ensure successful and effective training. It is crucial that every dog feels safe and comfortable during training sessions. When you start noticing signs of stress in your dog, such as lip smacking, yawning, or excessive panting, it's vital to investigate the potential triggers behind these behaviors, as highlighted by Overall (2013). According to Thompson et al. (2017), the first step is to identify these triggers and then adjust your training methods as needed to create a safe and comfortable training environment. Offering rewards, as suggested by Friedman (2010), and providing positive praise can foster trust and help reduce their stress.

If your dog continues to display stress signals or struggles to make progress even with these modifications, consider shortening training sessions to prevent mental fatigue, breaking down complex tasks into manageable steps to reduce anxiety, and offering frequent breaks to allow your dog to relax and decompress in a quiet, distraction-free environment. Sometimes, counterconditioning can be a useful technique to change your dog's emotional response by associating cues with positive experiences.

However, if your dog consistently shows signs of stress during training and doesn't respond to these modifications, it's advisable to seek the expertise of a professional dog trainer or behaviorist. They can provide personalized strategies to address your dog's unique needs and challenges.

Recognizing and responding to your dog's stress signals is essential for their emotional well-being. Your primary goal should always be trust-building with your canine, ensuring their comfort, and ultimately achieving training success. By adapting your training methods to alleviate stress and anxiety, you not only benefit the dog but also strengthen the bond between you and your furry companion. These skills contribute to a rewarding and stress-free training journey, fostering growth and well-being in dogs.

Vocal Communication from Your Dog

Canines employ three primary forms of vocal communication, namely barking, whining or whimpering, and growling. As elucidated by McConnell (2002), barking can manifest in various types such as alert barking, playful barking, or fear-based barking, with the underlying cause determined by the triggering stimulus.

Whining typically indicates distress, discomfort, or excitement, as noted by Donaldson (2008). As a trainer, it's essential to discern the context and respond appropriately to address the dog's needs effectively.

Growling, as suggested by Salman et al. (2000), often serves as a signal of discomfort, fear, or even playfulness. In such instances, it's crucial to investigate the specific situation and adapt your actions accordingly to ensure a positive and productive training experience.

Building Trust and Connection with Your Dog

One of the foundational elements in training your canine is the establishment of a strong bond with your dog through the cultivation of trust, as emphasized by Overall (2013). This trust serves as the cornerstone of the relationship between the dog and the trainer. Apply it with the use of positive reinforcement training to cultivate consistent success.

Positive Reinforcement Training

As you incorporate positive reinforcement methods into your training approach, it's essential to maintain consistency in both your training methods and the rewards you provide. Consistency in rewards fosters trust and a deeper understanding between you and your canine companion. Additionally, be patient throughout the training process, as training is a time-consuming endeavor. Demonstrating patience and avoiding punishment is crucial to preserving trust and building a strong bond with your dog. Always remember to reward your dog for their efforts and progress.

Physical Contact and Affection

Establishing effective communication with your dog is a key aspect of your relationship. Equally important is understanding how your dog communicates with you. Recognize that physical contact and affection can be a means of communication, strengthening the bond between humans and dogs or trainers. To begin, learn your dog's preferences for petting and grooming. Spending quality time together engaging in activities your dog enjoys reinforces your role as a source of joy and companionship. Consider play and interactive activities as opportunities for nurturing your connection, as play is a vital component of building a strong bond. Engage in games, fetch, or interactive toys to keep your dog mentally and physically engaged. If you prefer, incorporate training sessions into the bonding experience, as they too can be a form of play or interactive activity. Utilize training time to reinforce your relationship and build trust, contributing to the growth of your connection.

Understanding your dog's body language, actively listening to their cues, and establishing trust and connection are fundamental to effective training and a fulfilling relationship. By comprehending your dog's unique communication style and responding with empathy, you can establish a harmonious partnership rooted in mutual respect and trust.

In the upcoming chapter, we will delve into mastering recall and loose leash walking, enabling your dog to relish walks and outdoor activities while maintaining safety and control.

Heidi (age nine) our Honorary Grandma & eldest of the poodle pack of seven.

4

CHAPTER FOUR

Understanding Basic Obedience

Responsible pet ownership entails much more than providing food, shelter, and love to our four-legged companions. It extends to ensuring the safety, happiness, and well-being of our pets and those they interact with. A critical aspect of this responsibility is basic obedience dog training. It is the foundation upon which the house of harmony between pet and owner is built. Employing positive reinforcement techniques, maintaining consistency and patience, and considering professional guidance are essential elements of a successful training regimen, fostering well-behaved, safe, and content canine companions.

Basic obedience dog training is, at its core, an act of love and responsibility. It ensures that our pets are not only a joy to have around but also that they remain safe and do not pose a threat to themselves, other animals, or humans. A well-trained dog is less likely to engage in destructive behaviors, such as chewing on furniture, barking incessantly, or digging up the garden. More importantly, they are less prone to run off into dangerous situations, respond to commands promptly, and are generally more manageable in social settings. These attributes contribute to the safety and well-being of the dog, their owners, and the community at large.

The use of positive reinforcement techniques is one of the most humane and effective ways to train a dog. It is a process based on rewards, not punishments. When a dog behaves as desired, it receives a treat, praise, or a toy. This encourages the dog to repeat the behavior, fostering a sense of accomplishment and happiness. Positive reinforcement helps create a strong bond between the owner and the dog, promoting trust and mutual respect. When a dog is trained with kindness and rewards, it is more likely to be well-behaved and happy.

Consistency and patience are the cornerstones of a successful obedience training program. Dogs, like humans, do not learn instantly. Repetition and practice are required for them to grasp and internalize commands fully. For example, the "sit" command may take some time to learn, but with consistent and patient training, it becomes second nature to the dog. Staying calm and understanding the individual pace of the dog is vital to a harmonious training process. Inconsistency or impatience can lead to confusion and stress for the dog, ultimately undermining the effectiveness of the training.

While individual efforts are significant, considering professional guidance is a wise decision. Trained dog trainers and obedience classes offer specialized knowledge and insights into dog behavior. They can tailor training programs to address specific issues and provide guidance on handling challenges. A professional's expertise can significantly expedite the training process and ensure that commands are learned correctly and safely. Furthermore, professional trainers are well-equipped to address behavioral problems that may arise during training, preventing them from becoming persistent issues.

In conclusion, basic obedience dog training is not merely a suggestion for pet owners; it is a crucial responsibility. Employing positive reinforcement techniques, maintaining consistency and patience, and considering professional guidance are the essential pillars of a successful training regimen. These practices help create well-behaved, safe, and happy canine companions. By investing time, effort, and resources into training our dogs responsibly, we not only enhance their lives but also contribute to a safer and more harmonious coexistence within our communities. After all, a well-trained dog is a reflection of responsible and caring pet ownership.

Hank Jr. age one, looking dapper as always.

5

CHAPTER FIVE

Mastering the Dog Recall and Loose Leash Walking

In this chapter, we will explore essential aspects of dog training that enhance the safety and enjoyment of outdoor activities. We will delve into achieving a reliable recall, mastering loose leash walking, and using fun games to reinforce good behavior in your canine companion.

Achieving a Reliable Recall with a Dog

Recall, or coming when called, is a fundamental command that ensures your dog's safety and freedom during outdoor adventures. Achieving a reliable recall is essential for off-leash activities. On the following page we give you a step by step guide on how to train your dog to lean a reliable recall.

A Step-by-Step Guide:

Training for a Reliable Recall

Step 1: Start in a quiet, low-distraction environment.
Use a long leash for control and call your dog's name followed by the recall command ("Come"). Reward your dog with treats and praise when they come to you.

Step 2: Gradually increase distance between you and the dog.
Continue rewarding each successful recall.

Step 3: Begin to introduce controlled distractions.
As your dog becomes more reliable, introduce controlled distractions. Practice recalls around other dogs, people, or tempting scents.

Step 4: Begin Proofing.
As explained by Blackwell et al. (2008), this is the stage that you begin to perform what is called "proofing." Proofing involves practicing recall in diverse locations and situations to strengthen the reliability of the behavior.

Step 5: Use the same recall command and reward generously.
Make coming to you a positive experience. You can't give enough treats at this stage.

Enjoying Walks with Loose Leash Walking

Taking your dog for a walk should be a source of enjoyment for both you and your furry friend. The skill of loose leash walking, in which your dog walks calmly without pulling, can significantly enhance the pleasure of your strolls. Salman et al. (2000) underscored the importance of consistency in training and the practice of patience when aiming for successful loose leash walking.

If your dog is new to leash walking or still struggles with feeling comfortable during a walk, whether it's with a loose leash or any leash, this comprehensive guide is here to assist you.

Training Loose Leash Walking

Step 1: Choose a leash that suits your dog's size and strength.
A front-clip harness can help discourage pulling.

Step 2: Begin your walk.
When your dog walks without pulling, reward them with treats or praise. Use positive reinforcement to encourage this behavior.

Step 3: Stop if you dog starts to pull.
Wait for them to return to your side. Reward them when they do.

Step 4: Change direction frequently during walks.
This will keep your dog engaged and prevent pulling.

Fun Games to Reinforce Good Behavior

Integrating enjoyable and interactive games into your training regimen not only reinforces positive behavior but also deepens the connection between you and your dog. These games serve as a wonderful opportunity to infuse variety into your sessions and create a deeper, more meaningful bond between you and your canine companion.

Play Fetch

Engaging in a game of fetch is a fantastic method to provide exercise for your dog while practicing recall. Employ your dog's favorite ball or toy to infuse excitement into the game.

Step 1: Start in a controlled area and gradually increase the distance.

Step 2: (Recall) Incorporate recall into the game by calling your dog back to you before throwing the ball again.

Hide and Seek

Step 1: Hide from your dog and encourage them to find you. Use treats or a favorite toy to reward them when they locate you.

Step 2: (Recall and Search) Combine recall training with hide and seek by calling your dog to find you in various hiding spots.

Treasure Hunt

Step1: Hide treats or toys around your home or yard, and encourage your dog to search for them.

Step 2: (Scent Work) Engage your dog's sense of smell, providing mental stimulation and reinforcing their natural instincts.

Step-by-Step Guide:

Basic Obedience Tricks for Your Dog

Basic obedience tricks are fundamental for a well-behaved and happy dog. These tricks not only improve your dog's behavior but also strengthen the bond between you and your furry friend. In this step-by-step guide, we'll explore how to teach your dog some essential obedience tricks that form the foundation of good behavior.

Trick 1: "Sit" Command

Step 1: Prepare Treats.

Gather small, tasty treats that your dog loves. These treats will serve as rewards during training.

Step 2: Get Your Dog's Attention.

Find a quiet, distraction-free area to start training. Call your dog's name or use a clicker if you've trained them to respond to it.

Step 3: The Basic Position.

Stand in front of your dog with a treat in your hand. Hold the treat close to your dog's nose, but don't let them take it yet.

Step 4: Command and Gesture.

Say the command "Sit" while gently raising the treat above your dog's head and slightly moving it backward.

Step 5: Sitting Position.

As your dog follows the treat, they should naturally sit down. The moment their bottom touches the ground, reward them with the treat and lots of praise.

Step 6: Practice and Repeat.

Repeat the process several times. Gradually increase the duration of the sit before giving the treat. Always use positive reinforcement and lots of praise.

Trick 2: "Stay" Command

Step 1: Start with "Sit".

Begin with your dog in the sitting position.

Step 2: Command "Stay".

Hold your hand, palm facing your dog, in front of their face. Say the command "Stay" while taking a step back.

Step 3: Pause.

Pause for a few seconds while maintaining eye contact with your dog.

Step 4: Return and Reward.

Return to your dog and reward them with a treat and praise. Initially, keep the duration short and gradually increase it over time.

Step 5: Increase Distance.

As your dog becomes more comfortable with "Stay," gradually increase the distance between you and your dog.

Step 6: Practice and Release.

Practice the "Stay" command regularly, and always release your dog with a cue like "Okay" or "Free" when you're ready for them to move.

Trick 3: "Lie Down" Command

Step 1: Prepare Treats.

Gather your treats.

Step 2: Start with "Sit".

Begin with your dog in the sitting position.

Step 3: Command "Down".

Hold a treat close to your dog's nose.

Say the command "Down" while moving the treat down towards the ground.

Step 4: Lie Down.

As your dog follows the treat, they should lie down. Reward them with the treat and praise once they are fully down.

Step 5: Practice.

Practice the "Down" command regularly, and eventually, your dog will respond without needing a treat lure.

Trick 4: "Come" (Recall) Command

Step 1: Prepare Treats.

Gather your treats.

Step 2: Start in a Controlled Environment.
Begin training in a quiet, enclosed space to minimize distractions. Have your dog on a leash and collar.

Step 3: Command "Come".
Kneel or crouch down.

Call your dog's name followed by the command "Come."

Step 4: Encourage and Reward.
Gently encourage your dog to come to you with the leash if needed. As soon as your dog reaches you, reward them with a treat and lots of praise.

Step 5: Increase Distance.
Gradually increase the distance between you and your dog during recall training.

Step 6: Practice.
Practice the "Come" command regularly, in various environments and situations, to reinforce reliable recall.

Trick 5: "Leave It" Command

Step 1: Prepare Treats and an Object.
Have some treats in one hand and a small, safe object (like a toy) in the other hand.

Step 2: Present the Object.
Hold the object in your open hand, close to your dog's nose.

Step 3: Command "Leave It".

Say the command "Leave It" firmly but not harshly.

Step 4: Wait for Compliance.

Wait for your dog to stop trying to get the object or treat. When they back away or lose interest, reward them with a treat from your other hand.

Step 5: Repeat and Increase Difficulty.

Practice "Leave It" with various objects and gradually make it more challenging.

Step 6: Practice Self-Control.

Eventually, your dog should learn to leave things alone without a command.

Trick 6: "Down-Stay" (Combining Commands)

Step 1: Start with "Down" and "Stay".

Begin with your dog in the "Down" position.

Step 2: Command "Down-Stay".

Say the command "Down-Stay" while using the hand signal for "Stay."

Step 3: Pause.

Maintain eye contact and wait for a few seconds.

Step 4: Reward and Praise.

Return to your dog and reward them with a treat and praise for staying in the "Down" position.

Step 5: Increase Duration and Distance.
Gradually increase the duration and distance of the "Down-Stay" command.

Step 6: Practice.
Practice "Down-Stay" regularly in different environments and situations.

Teaching your dog basic obedience commands is a rewarding journey that enhances your dog's behavior and forges a stronger bond between you. Remember to maintain positivity in your training sessions, utilize treats and praise as rewards, and practice patience and consistency in delivering your commands. As your dog becomes proficient in these fundamental obedience tricks, you'll be better prepared to tackle more advanced behaviors, ensuring a well-behaved and joyful canine companion.

Acquiring a dependable recall, mastering loose leash walking, and incorporating enjoyable games into your training regimen are pivotal steps in enhancing your dog's outdoor experience while deepening the connection between you and your four-legged friend. These skills not only promote your dog's physical and mental well-being but also ensure that outdoor activities are safe and enjoyable for both of you.

In the forthcoming chapter, we will shift our focus to the critical importance of early socialization, fostering positive interactions with other dogs and people, and addressing behavioral challenges through the power of socialization.

Riley and his daughter Annabella, sister to Nala.

6

CHAPTER SIX

Understanding the importance of Canine Socialization

In this extensive chapter, we will explore the crucial role of socialization in a dog's life. We'll discuss the significance of early socialization, the benefits of positive encounters with other dogs and people, and how to address behavioral challenges through effective socialization techniques.

The Importance of Early Socialization

Early socialization is a vital component of a dog's development, setting the foundation for their behavior and temperament throughout their life. It is a process of exposing puppies to a variety of people, animals, environments, and experiences during their critical developmental period, typically between 3 weeks and 14 weeks of age [Overall, 2013].

Benefits of Early Socialization

During early development three weeks to fourteen weeks of age, puppies are particularly receptive to new experiences and stimuli. Proper socialization during this window can have a profound and lasting impact on a dog's behavior and attitude toward people, animals, and their environment. Early socialization has proven to not only help prevent behavioral problems but also lay the foundation for a more confident, well-adjusted, and more adaptable canine companion.

Reduced Fear and Aggression: Properly socialized dogs are less likely to develop fear-based behaviors or aggression towards unfamiliar people and dogs [Blackwell et al., 2008].

Confidence and Improved Adaptability: Early exposure to different environments and stimuli helps dogs adapt to new situations and reduces anxiety in unfamiliar settings. These well-socialized puppies developed stronger confidence and better adaptability than puppies without the socialization which made them better equipped to handle stressful situations throughout their life.

Enhanced Learning: Socialized dogs tend to be more receptive to training and learning new commands.

Strengthened Bond: Socialization experiences that are positive and enjoyable help strengthen the bond between you and your dog.

Better Communication Skills: Socialized puppies learn appropriate communication and body language, which helps prevent misunderstandings and conflicts in their interactions with other dogs and people.

Easier Handling and Veterinary Care: Dogs that are accustomed to handling and examination during early socialization are generally more cooperative and less stressed during veterinary visits and grooming.

Improved Quality of Life: Well-socialized dogs are more likely to be included in family activities, have greater freedom, and enjoy a higher quality of life.

How Well Socialized Is You Dog?

Effective socialization is a fundamental requirement for nurturing a well-adjusted and self-assured dog. It allows them to form favorable connections with people, animals, surroundings, and various encounters. We are going to use the checklist as both a quiz and a guide for this next part.

After reading through each section and receiving your score, utilize the Dog Socialization Checklist/Quiz as a valuable reference tool. This checklist serves as a helpful guide for prioritizing your dog's socialization skills, ensuring that their life is enriched with opportunities to interact with new people and explore novel experiences, just like humans. It's essential to avoid the scenario where your dog withdraws into a solitary existence, remaining at home and never venturing out, as this can lead to behavioral issues, anxiety, frustration, destructive chewing, boredom, and more.

Frequently, we witness owners enrolling their puppies in obedience or puppy manners classes. However, once their pups excel in these classes, what's the next step? Do they continue with advanced obedience training or embark on a journey to become trained support dogs? At times, they do, while at other times, owners discontinue their investment in their dogs' development. This is when behavioral issues can start to manifest. It can happen to the best of us—dogs developing a fear of the outside world or strangers. However, it's encouraging to note that owners are increasingly recognizing the myriad benefits dogs bring, including stress relief and the advantages of having them accompany us everywhere, leading to dogs experiencing more socialization than ever before.

Upon completing the quiz, I recommend setting a goal to address any unchecked boxes that pertain to your dog's socialization. By doing so, you essentially certify that you've comprehensively covered the essential facets of socializing your dog. This process not only improves your understanding of your dog but also highlights areas where they may need additional work.

If you encounter an item on the checklist that you believe you've addressed but your dog struggles with, such as the example of fireworks causing fear and hiding in their crate, make a note on the page, check it off, and continue. The objective is to uncover your pet's past experiences. During this process, you may identify behaviors issues or challenges separate from a dog who has been well socialized, that requires professional intervention from a certified dog trainer or behaviorist, which will be discussed in a later section of the book. Tally your score and see what you get.

Dog Socialization Quiz/Checklist

People

☐ Family Members: Ensure your dog is comfortable and well-socialized with all members of your household.

☐ Friends and Guests: Expose your dog to different friends and guests who visit your home.

☐ Children: If applicable, make sure your dog is comfortable around children of various ages.

☐ Strangers: Teach your dog to remain calm and friendly when meeting unfamiliar people in public places.

☐ Veterinary Staff: Familiarize your dog with veterinary visits and interactions with veterinarians and staff.

☐ Groomer or Pet Stylist: Socialize your dog to grooming procedures, including brushing, nail trimming, and bathing.

☐ Delivery Personnel: Help your dog remain relaxed when encountering delivery workers or mail carriers.

_____ **Total out of 7**

Other Dogs

☐ Playdates: Arrange playdates with other well-behaved dogs to promote positive interactions.

☐ Dog Parks: Visit dog parks to expose your dog to various breeds and play styles.

☐ Puppy Classes: Attend puppy socialization classes where your dog can interact with puppies of similar age.

- ☐ Obedience Classes: Enroll your dog in obedience classes to improve their social skills and behavior around other dogs.

- ☐ Leash Walks: Practice polite leash manners when encountering other dogs during walks.

______ **Total out of 5**

Environments

- ☐ Home: Ensure your dog is comfortable and confident in your home environment.

- ☐ Yard: Familiarize your dog with your yard and any outdoor areas they frequent.

- ☐ Parks: Visit different parks, trails, and outdoor spaces to expose your dog to diverse environments.

- ☐ Urban Settings: If applicable, socialize your dog to city or urban environments, including streets, sidewalks, and traffic.

- ☐ Indoor Public Places: Take your dog to pet-friendly stores, cafes, or indoor spaces where dogs are welcome.

______ **Total out of 5**

Experiences

- ☐ Car Rides: Make car rides a positive experience, as dogs may need to travel for various reasons.

- ☐ Elevators: Socialize your dog to riding in elevators, if necessary.

- ☐ Public Events: Attend pet-friendly events, fairs, or gatherings to expose your dog to crowds and new experiences.

- ☐ Outdoor Activities: Involve your dog in outdoor activities like hiking, picnics, or camping trips.

- ☐ Water: If your dog enjoys water, expose them to safe swimming experiences.

_______ **Total out of 5**

Objects and Sounds

- ☐ Household Objects: Familiarize your dog with common household objects, such as vacuum cleaners, appliances, and household items.

- ☐ Noises: Introduce your dog to various noises, including doorbells, sirens, thunder, and fireworks.

- ☐ Music and TV: Play music and TV shows at a reasonable volume to help your dog become accustomed to different sounds.

- ☐ Traffic: Train your dog to remain calm around traffic noises and vehicle sounds.

_______ **Total out of 4**

Handling and Care

- ☐ Grooming: Ensure your dog is comfortable with grooming activities, including brushing, ear cleaning, and nail trimming.

- ☐ Veterinary Exams: Teach your dog to tolerate and remain calm during veterinary examinations.

- ☐ Handling: Socialize your dog to being handled by different people, including checking their paws, mouth, and ears.

☐ Dental Care: Introduce your dog to regular dental care routines, such as teeth brushing.

☐ Ear Cleaning: Socialize your dog to having their ears cleaned as needed.

_____ **Total out of 5**

Miscellaneous

☐ New Experiences: Continuously expose your dog to new and novel experiences, people, and places to maintain socialization.

☐ Positive Reinforcement: Use treats, praise, and toys to reward and reinforce positive behavior during socialization.

☐ Stay Calm: Remain calm and confident during socialization encounters to help your dog feel at ease.

☐ Gradual Exposure: Introduce your dog to new experiences gradually, considering their comfort level.

☐ Respect Boundaries: Always respect your dog's boundaries and comfort zones, avoiding overwhelming situations.

______ **Total out of 5 Miscellaneous**

______ Total out of 7 People

______ Total out of 5 Other Dogs

______ Total out of 5 Environments

______ Total out of 5 Experiences

______ Total out of 4 Objects and Sounds

______ Total out of 5 Handling and Care

______ Total out of 5 Miscellaneous

______ Grand Total out of 36 How Social is your Pup?

| 33 and up | **Wow my dogs a socialite!**

| 25 and up | **Wow my dogs a social butterfly!**

| 15 and up | **My dogs social.**

| Under 14 | **My dogs a little social.**

| Under 7 | **Yes, my dog thinks he could be a little more social sometimes.**

How did your performance turn out? Were the results unexpected for you? Did you discover anything novel about yourself and your canine companion that perhaps eluded you previously? Feel free to jot down any observations below.

____

____

____

____

____

____

____

____

____

Consistent and positive socialization encounters are vital at every stage of your dog's life. Fostering their development into well-rounded, confident, and well-behaved companions can be fun and it is definitely rewarding. We have also included an additional socialization checklist in the back of the book to use. Please feel free to customize either checklist to suit your dog's individual needs and temperament. Should you encounter any specific challenges during the socialization process, please seek guidance from a professional dog trainer or certified behaviorist.

Tips for Positive Encounters

Creating positive encounters for dogs with others is essential for their social development and overall well-being. Whether your dog is meeting other dogs, people, or various animals, here are some tips to ensure these interactions are positive and enjoyable:

Start Early: Begin socialization when your dog is a puppy, ideally between the ages of three to fourteen weeks. Early exposure helps puppies build positive associations with various experiences.

Positive Reinforcement: Use treats, praise, and toys to reward and reinforce good behavior during encounters. This positive reinforcement encourages your dog to repeat the desired behavior.

Choose Appropriate Settings: Pick controlled and safe environments for socialization. Start in quieter settings and gradually expose your dog to more challenging situations as they become more comfortable.

Observe Body Language: Pay close attention to your dog's body language. Look for signs of relaxation (loose body, wagging tail) and stress (stiffness, lip licking, yawning). If your dog appears anxious or fearful, remove them from the situation and try again later.

Slow Introductions: When introducing your dog to new people or animals, take it slow. Allow them to approach at their own pace and don't force interactions.

Positive Associations: Pair new experiences with positive outcomes. For example, give treats and praise when your dog meets new people or animals. This helps create a positive association with the encounter.

Gradual Exposure: If your dog is fearful or reactive, gradually expose them to the trigger at a distance. As they become more comfortable, you can decrease the distance.

Controlled Playdates: Arrange playdates with known, well-behaved dogs. Ensure the dogs are of similar size and energy level to prevent intimidation or excessive rough play.

Proper Leash Etiquette: Maintain proper leash manners when walking your dog. Keep the leash loose and allow your dog to greet others in a controlled manner. Avoid tension on the leash, as it can create anxiety.

Consistency: Be consistent in your training and socialization efforts. Regular practice helps reinforce positive behavior.

Socialization Classes: Consider enrolling your dog in a reputable puppy socialization class or basic obedience class led by a professional trainer.

Supervision: Always supervise interactions with other dogs and people, especially in the early stages of socialization.

Set Realistic Expectations: Understand that not all encounters will be perfect. Some dogs may have preferences for certain individuals or animals. Focus on overall progress rather than expecting perfection in every interaction.

Avoid Overwhelming Situations: Be mindful of your dog's threshold for socialization. Avoid overwhelming them with too many new experiences or interactions in a short period.

Stay Calm: Dogs can sense your emotions. Stay calm and relaxed during socialization encounters to help your dog feel at ease.

Seek Professional Help: If your dog exhibits excessive fear, aggression, or reactivity, consult with a professional dog trainer or behaviorist for guidance and specialized training.

Remember that socialization is an ongoing process, and it's important to continue exposing your dog to various experiences throughout their life. With patience, positive reinforcement, and gradual exposure, you can help your dog become a well-adjusted and socially confident companion.

Addressing Behavioral Challenges through Socialization

Socialization is a critical aspect of a dog's upbringing, contributing significantly to their behavior, temperament, and overall well-being. While early socialization primarily focuses on positive encounters with people, other dogs, and various environments, it also plays a crucial role in addressing and preventing behavioral challenges in dogs. By systematically exposing your dog to stimuli that trigger problem behaviors, you can desensitize and counter condition them to respond differently.

The Significance of Socialization on Dog Behavior

Socialization encompasses the process of exposing a dog to a variety of individuals, animals, settings, and experiences during their early weeks and months of development. Effective socialization exerts a profound and lasting influence on a dog's behavior and outlook on life. It offers numerous advantages, such as reducing fear and anxiety, enhancing communication skills, boosting confidence and adaptability, and proven prevention of behavior issues.

As per Fox (1978), a well-socialized dog is less inclined to develop fear-based aggression or anxiety in response to strangers, other dogs, or unfamiliar situations. Socialized dogs acquire the ability to grasp appropriate communication and proper body language in canine interactions, which, in turn, diminishes misunderstandings and conflicts in their interactions with both dogs and people. Ultimately, this fosters heightened confidence and improved adaptability, equipping them to navigate new and unfamiliar environments more effectively. This, in turn, contributes to the prevention of a wide array of behavior problems, including aggression, fearfulness, and excessive barking.

Addressing Behavioral Challenges

When confronted with behavioral challenges, it's common to feel uncertain about the way forward. However, what we've discovered is that socialization serves not only as a proactive measure in preventing behavioral problems but also plays a vital role in tackling existing ones. Here are some prevalent behavioral challenges that can be effectively managed through the application of socialization:

Dealing with Fear and Anxiety

When your dog displays fear or anxiety in response to specific situations or objects, such as thunderstorms or vacuum cleaners, a gradual process of exposure and the formation of positive associations can assist in alleviating their fear. Inclusive socialization that exposes your dog to diverse environments and people can also contribute to reducing separation anxiety by enhancing their comfort with various situations and individuals.

Another effective approach is desensitization, where you progressively introduce the fear-inducing stimulus at a low intensity and gradually increase it over time. Additionally, you can employ counterconditioning, as suggested by Donaldson (2008), by pairing the presence of the stimulus with something your dog adores, such as treats or play, to establish positive associations.

Handling Dog Aggression

For dogs exhibiting aggression towards other dogs or people, controlled and positive socialization can play a role in modifying their behavior. However, it's crucial to exercise caution, as the severity of aggression can vary. It's always advisable to seek the guidance of a professional dog trainer or behaviorist experienced in handling aggression cases, especially if you lack experience in addressing this challenge.

It's indeed true that dogs with fear or aggression issues can benefit from controlled exposure to the triggers of their fear or aggression. Gradual exposure, where you introduce carefully managed interactions with calm and non-threatening dogs or people while employing positive reinforcement to reward calm and non-aggressive behavior during these interactions, can contribute to their progress in overcoming dog aggression. As highlighted by Overall (2013), a positive socialization experience has the potential to alter their emotional response and reduce reactivity.

Facing Leash Reactivity

Dogs demonstrating leash reactivity, such as barking and lunging at other dogs or people during walks, can also derive benefits from controlled socialization experiences. The application of positive reinforcement techniques aids in teaching them to maintain a calm and relaxed demeanor in the presence of such triggers.

Dealing with Excessive Vocalization

Dogs inclined to excessive barking can also reap the rewards of socialization. Socialization exposes them to various sounds and environments, contributing to their desensitization to noises and triggers. When combined with positive reinforcement, this approach can yield significant and positive outcomes.

Strategies for Addressing Behavioral Challenges through Socialization

Dealing with behavioral challenges through socialization necessitates a highly structured and patient approach. Our primary recommendation is to initiate the process by seeking guidance from a professional dog trainer or behaviorist who can assess the specific challenges your dog faces and formulate a customized socialization plan. Once the plan is devised, you can embark on its implementation. In many cases involving dogs with behavioral challenges, the solution involves a combination of positive reinforcement techniques to reward calm and appropriate behavior during socialization experiences. Reward-based training can facilitate a transformation in the dog's emotional response to triggers.

Another integral part of the plan may entail gradually exposing the dog to the triggers of their behavioral challenges under controlled conditions. This can encompass a gradual introduction to other dogs, people, or environments while closely monitoring their reactions. Additionally, techniques like desensitization and counterconditioning can be employed to modify the dog's emotional response to specific triggers. Associating the presence of these triggers with positive experiences can effectively reduce fear or reactivity, as noted by Overall (2013).

Regular and Varied Socialization

Regular socialization for dogs typically involves exposing them to a consistent set of people, animals, environments, and experiences on an ongoing basis. This routine and structured approach can help dogs become familiar with and comfortable in their everyday surroundings and with the individuals and situations they frequently encounter. It's an important part of ensuring a well-adjusted and confident dog but may not encompass a wide range of diverse experiences.

On the other hand, varied socialization is a more comprehensive approach that exposes dogs to a wide range of people, animals, environments, and experiences, including those they might not encounter regularly. Varied socialization seeks to broaden a dog's comfort zone and prepare them to adapt to new and unexpected situations. It's a more extensive effort to ensure that dogs are not only well-adjusted in their familiar environment but also capable of handling novel and diverse experiences without undue stress or fear. Varied socialization is especially beneficial for creating adaptable and confident dogs that can thrive in a variety of circumstances.

The Role of Responsible Pet Owners

The role of a responsible pet owner is to offer consistency and ongoing socialization through training and education, employing a tailored approach that suits the specific needs of their dog. Socialization is not confined to a puppy's critical period (puppyhood) but should continue throughout their lifetime. Responsible pet owners should expose their dogs to new experiences and reinforce positive behaviors as they age. Educating oneself about the principles and techniques of early socialization is crucial, and professional guidance from experienced trainers can be highly valuable.

As a pet owner, you spend the most time with your dog, understanding their preferences and aversions. You are their greatest advocate in devising a customized plan that suits their individual requirements. It is vital to acknowledge the unique needs and sensitivities of each puppy, as not all puppies are alike, and socialization should be tailored to their distinct personalities. Responsible pet ownership extends beyond socialization, encompassing wellness. Regular veterinary checkups are essential to ensure that the puppy remains healthy and free from illness during socialization activities.

Addressing behavioral challenges through socialization is a proactive and effective approach to enhancing a dog's behavior, temperament, and overall quality of life, representing a fundamental aspect of responsible pet ownership. Adequate socialization during the critical period for socialization provides an exceptional opportunity to mold a puppy's future by exposing them to diverse experiences in a positive and secure manner. It not only prevents behavioral issues but also plays a crucial role in addressing existing challenges such as fear, aggression, leash reactivity, separation anxiety, and excessive vocalization.

By introducing puppies to a variety of people, animals, environments, and experiences, responsible pet owners lay the foundation for raising well-adjusted and confident canine companions. Positive interactions with other dogs and people further promote good social behavior, while socialization can also serve as a tool to tackle behavioral challenges when necessary. The benefits of early socialization, including increased confidence, reduced fear, and improved communication skills, underscore its importance in nurturing well-adjusted and well-behaved canine companions.

Responsible pet owners assume a vital role in early socialization, commencing the process as early as possible, continuing it throughout their dog's life, and adapting the approach to meet their puppy's individual needs. By grasping the principles of effective socialization and prioritizing their dog's well-being, owners ensure that their canine companions mature into confident, adaptable, and content members of the family.

When the situation calls for it, consulting with professionals, implementing gradual exposure, employing positive reinforcement, and utilizing desensitization and counterconditioning techniques, pet owners can assist their canine companions in overcoming behavioral challenges and evolving into confident, well-adjusted, and cheerful members of the family. Remember, socialization is an ongoing process that continues throughout a dog's life, ensuring their adaptability and responsiveness to a variety of situations and environments.

In the next chapter, we will delve into positive approaches to common behavioral issues, crafting behavior modification plans, and the essential qualities of patience and persistence in training.

Roxanne mother to Nala and Annabella shown above
And a member of the poodle crew.

7

CHAPTER SEVEN

Utilizing Behavior Modification

In this comprehensive chapter, we will explore positive approaches to addressing common behavioral issues in dogs, creating behavior modification plans tailored to individual needs, and the vital qualities of patience and persistence required for successful training.

Effective Dog Training and Behavioral Modification

Effective dog training involves not only teaching commands but also addressing behavioral issues that may arise throughout a dog's life. Common behavioral problems include separation anxiety, aggression, excessive barking, and destructive behavior. This chapter will delve into positive approaches for dealing with these issues, emphasizing science-based methods and humane training techniques.

Tackling Canine Behavioral Issues:
A Comprehensive Approach

Behavioral issues in dogs can be challenging for both pet owners and their furry companions. The importance of a positive approach, early intervention, and professional guidance are all keys to tackling the issues successfully. However the Initial steps begin by first prioritizing health and seeking professional guidance when faced with behavioral issues in your dog.

It is always recommended to begin with a thorough consideration of health-related factors that might contribute to these behaviors. Promptly consulting your veterinarian is highly advisable, as they can help rule out any underlying issues ranging from pain and illness to potential disorders. Again, ensuring your dog's physical well-being is the first step toward addressing behavioral concerns.

Once your veterinarian confirms your dog's health and well-being, the next course of action is to seek guidance from a qualified animal behaviorist. These professionals are well-equipped to provide advice on effective techniques and offer tailored support to address your dog's specific needs.

Understanding and Addressing Separation Anxiety

Separation anxiety is a prevalent issue in dogs, often leading to destructive behavior and distress for both the owner and the dog. This condition becomes apparent when your dog experiences extreme stress from the moment you leave them alone until your return, often displaying symptoms resembling a deep fear of being alone in the house.

Recognizing Separation Anxiety: Symptoms and Triggers

Symptoms of separation anxiety can vary widely, with no single defining indicator. While a single symptom, especially if infrequent, may not necessarily point to separation anxiety, consistent display of multiple symptoms is a strong indicator. Common behaviors associated with separation anxiety include anxious pacing, whining, trembling, excessive barking or howling, destructive acts like chewing or digging, indoor accidents, and excessive salivation, drooling, or panting. Some dogs may make desperate and prolonged attempts to escape confinement, often leading to injury.

Potential triggers for separation anxiety include lack of prior experience being left alone, traumatic separations (common in some abandoned shelter dogs), or even a single traumatic event during the owner's absence, such as a house break-in. Personality traits, with clingy dogs potentially at greater risk than independent ones, may also play a role. Major life changes, such as a sudden shift in routine, moving to a new home, or the sudden absence of a family member due to divorce, death, or a child leaving for college, can also trigger or exacerbate separation anxiety.

Treatment and Management

Dealing with separation anxiety can be a challenging and an emotionally taxing experience. However, there are several steps pet owners can take to address this issue effectively. Some of the treatment methods align with preventive measures that may already be part of your dog's routine. These include:

Crate Training: Introducing a crate properly to provide your dog with a secure and comfortable space associated with positive experiences, such as chew toys and food puzzles.

Desensitization and Counter-Conditioning: Gradually acclimating your dog to periods of alone time and making departures less distressing by associating them with high-value treats.

Exercise: Regular physical and mental exercise can help treat and prevent separation anxiety. Engaging your dog's mind with training sessions, puzzle toys, and cognitive games is essential.

Encouraging Independence: Teaching your dog to be comfortable in another room and to stay in place even when you're at home. Avoiding excessive emotional reactions when leaving or returning can help your dog remain calm.

Medication and Natural Supplements: In severe cases, medication or natural supplements may be necessary. Consulting your vet for advice on prescription medication or natural remedies like CBD or valerian are crucial.

Addressing behavioral issues in dogs requires a multifaceted approach that prioritizes the health and well-being of the animal, while also seeking professional guidance when necessary, and employing positive techniques to address specific problems like separation anxiety. With patience, and a positive attitude, including the right strategies in place, pet owners can effectively manage these issues, improving their dogs' well-being and enhancing the human-dog bond.

Managing Dog Separation Anxiety: Strategies & Approaches

Dog separation anxiety is a challenging and distressing behavioral problem that can affect both dogs and their owners. Dogs suffering from separation anxiety often exhibit disruptive behaviors, and pet owners face the dilemma of finding effective ways to help their pets feel comfortable and secure when left alone. Managing this condition requires a combination of approaches, including behavior modification and, in severe cases, medication. The choice of the most suitable method depends on the dog's individual needs and the duration of time they spend alone. We will explore various approaches to address dog separation anxiety, providing insights for pet parents seeking to alleviate this common issue.

Crate Training

One effective strategy to manage separation anxiety is crate training, which can counteract common misconceptions about crates. When done correctly, this technique helps dogs associate the crate with positive experiences and safety. It's important to introduce the crate gradually, allowing dogs to become comfortable with it and without prolonged periods of solitude. Over time, the crate can become a secure space where the dog feels protected, easing their anxiety when alone.

Behavior Modification

Systematic desensitization and counterconditioning are proven methods for reducing separation-related behavior problems in dogs. These techniques require guidance from veterinary behaviorists, who can help pet owners understand and implement them effectively. Both methods aim to make the dog less reactive to stress triggers, such as departure cues, and change the way the dog perceives these cues. By gradually acclimating the dog to separation, these methods help build resilience and reduce anxiety.

Dog-Appeasing Pheromones

Pheromones are natural chemicals that can induce a sense of calm in dogs. Female dogs release them to comfort newborn puppies, and these pheromones are available in various forms for pet owners, such as collars and diffusers. By using products infused with dog-appeasing pheromones, pet parents can help alleviate their dogs' distress when they leave. This approach can be particularly beneficial for those who find it difficult to say goodbye to their furry companions.

Calming Vests & Beds

Calming vests and beds provide an additional tool to help dogs manage their anxiety during times of stress. Vests work by applying gentle pressure to specific points on the dog's body, similar to the calming effect of swaddling on infants. Calming beds are designed to envelop the dog's body, creating a sense of security and comfort. These products can offer relief and elevate the dog's mood, making them feel safer when left alone.

Anti-Anxiety Supplements

The modern pet market offers a variety of supplements that promote calmness and relaxation in dogs. Most of these supplements are natural and safe for long-term use. Some popular choices include CBD oil, passionflower, chamomile, L-theanine, L-tryptophan, and B-complex vitamins. These supplements can be integrated into a dog's daily routine to help manage separation anxiety effectively.

Anti-Anxiety Medications

In severe cases of separation anxiety, veterinarians and behaviorists may recommend anti-anxiety medications. While these medications can be efficient in managing the condition, they come with potential side effects and are not suitable for long-term use. It's crucial for pet owners to consult their trusted veterinarian before administering any medication to their dogs. Medications should be considered as a last resort when other methods have proven ineffective.

Dog separation anxiety can be a distressing experience for both dogs and their owners. However, by implementing a combination of strategies and approaches, pet parents can effectively manage this condition and provide their dogs with a sense of security and comfort them when left alone. The choice of the most suitable method depends on the individual dog's needs, but with patience, dedication, and guidance from professionals, separation anxiety can often be successfully alleviated, improving the well-being of both the dog and their owner.

Handling Aggression in Dogs

While dog owners undoubtedly adore their furry companions, canine aggression ranks as a prominent concern when it comes to problematic behavior. Despite thousands of years of domestication, our canine friends occasionally exhibit behaviors that might be adaptive in the wild but are less than ideal for cohabiting with humans. Understanding these behaviors and their underlying origins is crucial for devising and adhering to a plan to minimize these problematic tendencies. There are numerous potential triggers contributing to aggression in dogs. Some dogs display aggression in various contexts, while others exhibit it only in specific circumstances. Generally, the potential triggers of dog aggression can be categorized into five main groups: fear, possessiveness, frustration, dominance, and pain/illness.

Fear is a common driver of aggression in dogs. When confronted with a frightening situation, dogs typically experience a "fight or flight response." If a dog feels cornered or trapped in such situations, fear aggression may manifest. Possessive behavior can also provoke aggression. Dogs may become aggressive when they are deeply protective of their food, treats, toys, resting spots, home, or even family members, viewing any potential threat to these possessions as a trigger.

Frustration can lead to aggression in dogs. Dogs left tethered outdoors for extended periods, unable to interact with passing humans and animals, can become overly agitated. This heightened state of arousal may escalate into aggression. Frustration-related aggression can occur in chained dogs as well as dogs restrained on a leash or within a fenced yard.

Dominance, though widely discussed, is actually less common as a cause of dog aggression than one might think. Dominance aggression occurs when a dog perceives a challenge to their position in the social hierarchy and responds aggressively to assert their "top dog" status. However, this is a relatively limited issue among dogs.

Aggression induced by pain or illness is perhaps the most straightforward to understand. Just as humans might be irritable when unwell, dogs can exhibit aggression if they are in pain or feeling unwell.

Understanding these prevalent causes of canine aggression can provide a foundation for addressing aggression issues in your dog.

Dogs exhibiting aggression on walks can significantly benefit from professional assistance, especially in severe cases when the dog is challenging to control. However, there are steps you can take at home if the dog's aggression is mild enough and you can safely manage it.

Start by focusing on basic obedience training, ensuring your dog responds reliably to commands like sit, stay, lie down, and come. Work on these commands in a controlled environment before progressing to more distracting settings. Once your dog consistently obeys these commands, you can use them to divert your dog's attention when encountering other dogs during walks. A well-trained dog can't bark or lunge at other dogs while sitting quietly and anticipating a treat.

Bear in mind that this method is unlikely to work when another dog is in very close proximity. Instead, initiate this training when the other dog is at a distance, with the assistance of a friend or neighbor. Have your friend stand with their dog at a substantial distance and ask your dog to obey a command. If your dog complies, reward them with a treat. Gradually decrease the distance between your dog and the other dog, repeating the process. Cease the training session when your dog struggles to obey. With consistent practice, your dog should eventually remain obedient even when another dog is nearby.

Dealing with dog aggression can be challenging and may require professional intervention, especially if the aggression occurs within the home. Inter-dog aggression among housemates is a serious matter that can result in injuries to dogs and even their owners. If your dog's exhibit significant aggression toward each other, take immediate steps to keep them separated at all times to prevent further conflicts. Consult your veterinarian for a referral to a veterinary behaviorist or a high-quality trainer who can assist in managing this problem.

Dogs employ barking as a form of communication, but excessive barking can be a nuisance. Common reasons for barking include territorial or alarm barking (directed at potential intruders) and attention-seeking. To manage territorial barking, limit your dog's view of the outside by closing blinds or using covered crates. You can also teach your dog a command like "quiet" or "go to your spot" to stop barking.

When dealing with attention-seeking barking, avoid reinforcing the behavior. Ignore your dog completely when they bark – don't yell, make eye contact, or engage. Wait until your dog stops barking before offering attention. Over time, most dogs learn that barking does not result in attention.

Jumping up is a common behavior among excited dogs during greetings. To discourage this behavior, don't reward your dog by giving them attention when they jump up. Instead, completely ignore them by turning away and walking away. Wait for your dog to calm down and sit, then reward them with attention. Over time, your dog will understand that jumping leads to being ignored, while sitting results in receiving the attention they seek.

Chewing is a natural dog behavior that can become problematic when it involves your possessions. To address this, move valuable items to inaccessible areas, and provide a variety of dog chew toys, including plastic or nylon bones and edible chews. Ensure supervision to prevent choking hazards. Over time, you'll learn which toys your dog prefers, and you can reintroduce your valuables once they consistently choose their toys over your belongings.

In dealing with any behavior problem, consistency is key. After identifying the issue and its underlying cause, develop a behavior plan that everyone in your household can consistently enforce. Consistency is crucial for correcting your dog's behavior issues, whether it's aggression or other problem behaviors.

To Do Checklist When Working with an Aggressive Dog

☐ Begin with a thorough vet examination to rule out any health-related causes of aggression.

☐ Seek guidance from a certified dog behavior consultant for professional insight.

☐ Implement desensitization and counterconditioning training as appropriate.

☐ Ensure your dog receives sufficient exercise and engages in enriching activities.

☐ Maintain a calm and composed demeanor when interacting with your pet.

☐ Utilize positive reinforcement and reward-based training methods.

☐ If your dog exhibits biting tendencies or there's suspicion of it, consider using a muzzle.

☐ Create a safe training environment to set your dog up for success.

☐ Address or eliminate triggers that may provoke aggression, such as providing more space during meals and addressing underlying anxiety.

☐ Employ management tools like puppy gates to separate your dog from people and other dogs when necessary.

☐ If advised by your vet or behaviorist, contemplate spaying or neutering your dog, especially if the aggression appears to be related to their sex.

First Step When Dealing with an Aggressive Dog: Get a Veterinarian to complete an exam first.

Dealing with aggression in dogs, regardless of their size, is a serious issue that should not be underestimated. Resolving this problem demands significant time, effort, and patience, as well as professional assistance. The first step when addressing an aggressive dog is scheduling a comprehensive veterinary examination, with an emphasis on discussing your concerns about aggression. Dogs, like humans, can become more irritable when they are in pain or not feeling well, which can often lead to aggressive behavior. If a medical issue is the root cause of your dog's aggression, training alone is unlikely to be effective. Therefore, a thorough physical examination is crucial, even if your dog doesn't display obvious signs of discomfort. Once your dog's health is confirmed, it's essential to consult with a certified canine behavioral consultant to address the aggression issue effectively.

Second Step is Considering Help from a Certified Behaviorist.

Resolving aggression in dogs is a complex challenge, often rooted in underlying issues. It is crucial to engage a certified dog behavior consultant, distinct from an ordinary dog trainer, to accurately assess the reasons behind your dog's aggressive behavior. These experts can craft a behavior modification plan tailored to your dog's specific issues, whether stemming from over arousal, fear, or anxiety.

Aggressive dogs pose a safety risk to you, your pet, and others. Therefore, it is imperative to have a certified canine behavioral consultant evaluate your aggressive dog before implementing any training or management regimen. It cannot be emphasized enough that you should work exclusively with a certified dog behavior expert, as most dog trainers lack the expertise required to address aggressive dog behavior, and well-intentioned but inexperienced trainers may inadvertently worsen the situation.

Safety is paramount when dealing with aggressive dogs, not only to prevent injuries to humans but also to safeguard the dog's life. In some cases, aggressive dogs may need to be euthanized, making caution and professional guidance vital in addressing these issues.

Third Step is When You Will Need to Assess If Your Dog is Getting Enough Exercise.

To address your dog's aggression, one of the initial steps is to ensure that your furry friend is living a fulfilling and happy life. This involves providing your dog with high-quality food, regular exercise, and ample mental stimulation. Neglecting these aspects can lead to emotions like depression and frustration, which may exacerbate aggressive behavior or even be a contributing factor.

Assess whether your dog's needs are being met by asking yourself a few key questions. Is your dog getting enough exercise, as most adult dogs typically require around an hour of light exercise each day? High-drive or high-energy dogs may need even more. It's important to engage your dog in outdoor activities to allow exploration and playtime.

In addition to exercise, make sure your dog receives enough playtime, which doesn't necessarily require interaction with other dogs; playing with you can be equally enjoyable. Regular 5-10 minute play sessions with your dog's favorite toys are recommended.

Mental enrichment is equally vital for your dog's well-being. Dogs need opportunities to practice their natural instincts and exercise their brains. Various enrichment activities can help, such as snuffle mats, frozen Kong filled with treats, lick mats, chews, shredding activities, and scavenger hunts. These activities not only engage your dog's mind but also help alleviate stress and anxiety.

By focusing on your dog's physical and mental health, you can create a more harmonious environment while awaiting professional assistance to address their aggression.

Step Four is When You Begin Management Techniques to Address Your Dogs Aggression.

Management techniques in dealing with an aggressive dog involve strategies to control their aggressive behavior, rather than modifying the behavior itself. These techniques are used to prevent further escalation of aggressive actions and to ensure the safety of both the dog and others. While it is best to use management techniques alongside behavior modification guided by a professional expert, they can be incredibly helpful when immediate assistance is challenging to obtain.

Examples of management techniques for aggressive dogs include indoor dog gates, which are versatile tools that can prevent a dog from escaping the house or protect them during mealtime or when guests are over. Crates can also be used to confine the dog temporarily, but they are not suitable for long periods of time.

Leashing an aggressive dog is essential when in public to ensure control and prevent any unwanted incidents. Muzzles are fool-proof tools to prevent dogs from biting and are a safety measure for everyone involved. Additionally, using "Do Not Pet" gear, such as harnesses, leashes, or bandanas, can help keep strangers and children from approaching the dog, particularly when dealing with breeds not typically associated with aggression.

It's crucial to evaluate the severity of your dog's aggressive behaviors, including growling, lunging, and biting. These actions represent the final stages of the canine ladder of aggression, indicating that the dog has been feeling stressed or anxious for a while. Understanding your dog's body language and recognizing even subtle cues is vital in addressing aggressive behaviors effectively.

Step Five Read and Learn About Dog Body Language.

We discuss this throughout the book but dogs communicate with their bodies. They don't have the luxury of using their words to tell us what is bothering them. We touch on the indicators of stress through body language but I think for the sake of clarity it's important to share with you common indicators of stress. These are:

- Yawning or nose licking

- Shifting focus away from you

- Angling body away

- Retreating

- Ears turning back

- Standing crouched with the tail tucked between legs

- Stiffening or tensing up

- Whale eyeing (showing the whites of eyes)

- Unbreakable stare

- Baring teeth

- Growling

- Harsh barking

- Lunging or charging

- Snapping

- Biting

Dogs will most often give plenty of warning before biting. Remember don't react or punish your dog. This can worsen the issue and put you at unnecessary risk.

Step Six Discuss with a Behaviorist Exactly Why Your Dog is Displaying Aggression.

Understanding the various types of dog aggression is crucial when addressing your dog's behavior issues, and it's essential to collaborate with a canine behaviorist and your veterinarian to identify the root causes. While the term "aggression" is often used, it's important to recognize that dogs exhibiting such behavior are often acting defensively, trying to create space between themselves and a perceived threat or discomfort.

Common triggers for aggressive behavior in dogs include fear, which can lead to fight or flight responses; anxiety, which is a more generalized emotion that can trigger aggression similar to fear; illness, as dogs may become grumpy or irritable when not feeling well; resource guarding, where dogs protect their prized possessions like food, bones, or toys; lack of stimulation and exercise, leading to frustration and irritability; sex-related aggression, often occurring in unaltered dogs during sexual situations; and idiopathic aggression, a rare and unpredictable form of aggression with an unknown cause.

Many of these aggression triggers can be prevented through proper training and socialization during puppyhood. However, traumatic experiences may set back progress, requiring a return to the basics later in life. This is a normal part of a dog's development, and it's important not to panic or feel guilty but to reset and move forward positively in addressing your dog's behavior.

Step Seven Read and Learn the Difference Between Aggression and Reactivity in a Dog.

Aggression and reactivity in dogs are often misunderstood and confused, but they have distinct differences. Reactivity refers to dogs who overreact to various stimuli, usually due to extreme sensitivity stemming from trauma, lack of socialization as puppies, or genetics. Common triggers for reactive dogs can include people, other dogs, loud noises, or even objects like bicycles and scooters. It's essential to recognize that some dogs may be reactive in specific situations, such as leashed walks, while remaining calm in other contexts.

Reactive dogs may display aggressive behavior when confronted with their triggers, leading some to label them as "aggressive dogs." However, many reactive dogs are affectionate and gentle in their home environments. On the other hand, truly aggressive dogs are in a constant state of stress and agitation, often due to fear, stress, frustration, or pain. Their aggression is not tied to a particular trigger and can happen at any time.

Understanding whether your dog is reactive or generally aggressive is crucial when implementing training and management strategies. Reactive dogs may benefit from desensitization training, while aggressive dogs require a more comprehensive approach that identifies the root causes of their behavior. It's important to avoid exposing your dog to triggers, as practicing unwanted behavior reinforces it. Keeping distance from triggers and using counter-conditioning and desensitization techniques can help reduce reactivity and aggression, ensuring the well-being of both the dog and their owner.

Step Eight Consider Purchasing a Muzzle.

Muzzles are invaluable tools when dealing with aggression in dogs, allowing them to safely interact in public and enjoy outdoor walks without posing a risk to others. They are essential for any owner of an aggressive dog and can be a real game-changer in ensuring safety. Basket-style muzzles are highly recommended as they allow dogs to pant, drink, and even take treats, such as the Baskerville muzzle.

Muzzles that completely close a dog's mouth should be avoided, as they are only suitable for very short periods and are typically used by groomers. Muzzles can also be useful for dogs that are not necessarily aggressive but are untested or inexperienced with specific populations, such as small children. They provide peace of mind in situations where potential mishaps could occur.

While it may be disheartening to put your dog in a muzzle, it is the most reliable way to prevent biting incidents. It's important to note that muzzles require some preparation and should not be suddenly strapped onto a dog, as this can cause fear and distress. Proper desensitization and training are necessary to ensure your dog is comfortable and cooperative with wearing a muzzle.

Step Nine Remember Not to Punish an Aggressive Dog.

When dealing with an aggressive dog, it's vital to avoid using punishment or aversive-based practices, including prong collars, e-collars, and leash corrections, alpha rolls, yelling, or scolding. Aggressive behaviors in dogs often stem from fear or anxiety, and these force-based methods can exacerbate fear, harm the relationship between you and your dog, and escalate an already tense situation.

The outdated notion of dogs displaying aggression to establish dominance as the "alpha dog" has been debunked and is not based on sound science. Instead, the focus should be on helping your dog feel safe, building their confidence, and using redirection, positive reinforcement, and counter-conditioning to address their behavior issues. Consulting with a certified dog behavior expert can be highly beneficial in formulating a plan that aligns with these goals. It's essential to avoid self-titled, non-certified behaviorists who suggest fear or pain-based tools, as long-term use of such methods can worsen aggression and lead to severe consequences, potentially resulting in the need for euthanasia.

Additionally, it's crucial never to punish a growling dog. Growling is a clear warning signal that dogs use to communicate their discomfort or unease. Punishing a dog for growling can lead them to skip this warning and resort to biting, as they learn that they get in trouble for growling. Allowing a dog to communicate through growling is essential for their well-being, as it indicates when they are feeling nervous, scared, or uncomfortable, giving them an alternative to resorting to more severe forms of aggression.

Step Ten Are Additional Techniques to Consider after You've Done Everything Else.

Dealing with an aggressive dog driven by fear, anxiety, and stress requires a thoughtful approach and a few key considerations. It's important to give your dog space at times, as these dogs can be easily overwhelmed and may benefit from occasional time alone.

Don't hesitate to explore behavior medications, which can be discussed with your veterinarian or canine behavior specialist. Medications like Xanax or Prozac can help reduce stress, and natural treatments such as aromatherapy supplements or CBD products may also be worth considering.

Additionally, tight-fitting compression garments like Thunder shirts, nutritional supplements including Omega-3 and vitamins (after consulting with your vet), and legal protection measures like extra insurance coverage, warning signs, security cameras, and high fences can help ensure your safety and your dog's well-being.

Remember that your dog is more than their aggression, and it's essential to relieve the pressure of expecting perfect behavior at all times. Take the necessary steps to ensure safety for yourself, your dog, and others. Aggression in dogs can be managed and improved through ongoing behavior modification and proper support, making it a workable challenge with the right guidance and tools.

Handling Excessive Barking

Barking is one of the primary means of vocal communication for dogs, and it can convey various messages depending on the context. Recognizing and comprehending the reasons behind a dog's barking is essential for fostering effective communication and addressing behavioral issues. Here, we outline the common motivations behind a dog's barking and provide guidance on how to manage excessive barking:

Territorial/Protective Barking

Dogs may bark excessively when they perceive a person or animal entering an area they consider their territory. This form of barking often escalates as the perceived threat gets closer, accompanied by alert body language.

Alarm/Fear Barking

Some dogs bark at any sudden noise or object that captures their attention or startles them. This type of barking can occur anywhere, not just within their territory, and is often accompanied by fearful body language.

Boredom/Loneliness Barking

Dogs are social animals and can become bored or lonely when left alone for extended periods, leading to excessive barking.

Barking may be a sign of unhappiness and a desire for stimulation.

Greeting/Play Barking

Dogs frequently bark when they are excited to greet people or other animals, usually in a friendly and happy manner.

This barking is often accompanied by tail wagging and may involve jumping.

Attention-Seeking Barking

Dogs may bark to get your attention and request something, such as going outside, playing, or receiving a treat.

Separation Anxiety/Compulsive Barking

Dogs with separation anxiety often bark excessively when left alone, accompanied by other symptoms like pacing, destructiveness, and depression. Compulsive barkers seem to bark without a specific trigger and may exhibit repetitive movements.

Managing Excessive Barking

Effectively addressing excessive barking in dogs requires time, patience, and consistent efforts.

Here are some tips to help you manage and reduce your dog's barking:

- Avoid shouting, as it can stimulate more barking. Use a calm and firm tone.

- Train your dog to understand the command "Quiet." When your dog barks, say "Quiet" in a calm voice, wait for them to stop barking (even briefly), then praise and reward them.

- Ensure your dog gets plenty of physical and mental exercise to alleviate boredom.

- Address barking issues promptly, as prolonged barking can become ingrained and lead to aggressive behavior.

- Consult a veterinarian to rule out any underlying medical issues causing excessive barking.

- Modify the environment to reduce triggers for territorial/protective or alarm/fear barking, such as using solid barriers or limiting access to windows.

- Combat boredom and loneliness by providing companionship or engaging activities.

- Train your dog to stay in a designated spot when someone arrives, eliminating the need for frenzied barking during greetings.

- Avoid rewarding barking by fulfilling your dog's requests only when they are calm.

- Seek professional help for separation anxiety or compulsive barking, as these issues may require behavioral therapy or medication.

- Be cautious with bark collars, as they may not be effective or could harm your dog.

It's crucial to manage your dog's barking in a humane and effective manner, considering their individual needs and triggers. By addressing the root causes and providing proper training and care, you can work toward a quieter and happier life for both you and your canine companion. Remember, understanding and patience are key in this journey.

Techniques for Addressing Excessive Barking

Identify Triggers: First, you will want to determine the cause or causes of the excessive barking (e.g., boredom, fear, or excitement). Once you determine the cause you can begin to address the root issue.

Provide Training and Enrichment: According to Landsberg et al., (2013) the best way to provide training and enrichment is through the use of positive reinforcement. Consider teaching the "Quiet" command and provide additional mental and physical enrichment to your do to reduce boredom.

Creating a Behavior Modification Plan

Behavior modification plans are essential tools for addressing and modifying unwanted behaviors effectively. These plans involve a systematic approach to identify triggers, set goals, and implement strategies to achieve desired outcomes [Friedman, 2010]. Your initial step should be gaining a comprehensive understanding of the target behavior. You need to begin by asking yourself, what precisely is the behavior in question? How frequently does it happen? Where it is typically observed? Can the pet owner provide insights on the behavior's intensity and frequency? Then, assess whether the problematic behavior poses any risks to the pet, other animals, or people. This information is crucial to creating your behavior modification plan and measuring the success of the treatment.

Start by engaging in a conversation with the owner about what the desired behavior should look like. It's important to differentiate between halting the problematic behavior and instilling a new, appropriate behavior. This discussion should shift the focus away from the issue at hand and emphasize the ideal behavior. Understand the client's expectations for change, evaluate their realism, and determine the necessary steps to attain these goals. Remember that a well-designed treatment plan is only effective if it aligns with the owner's needs, expectations, and their ability to implement it.

While you work on teaching new behaviors, be ready to offer management solutions for the specific problematic behavior. This behavior often strains the bond between humans and animals, leading to tension and, at times, punitive measures, which can further strain the relationship. Once you have implemented effective management, you can start training for alternative behaviors. Keep in mind that some owners may opt to manage the problem behavior rather than replace it with a new one.

When designing a treatment plan, consider that your ability to influence a pet's behavior might surpass the average pet owner's capabilities. Veterinarians typically have experience with a greater number of pets than the average client, allowing them to discern subtle behavioral changes and respond accordingly. However, it's essential to start with simple, incremental steps that approximate the final desired behavior. This involves establishing clear and predictable communication between the owner and the pet while recognizing that pets, as sentient beings, should have the capacity to decline certain requests.

Most behavior modification plans commence with foundational exercises. These small tasks impart basic control, calm behavior, and attentiveness to both the pet and the owner. Training sessions should be kept brief, focusing on teaching individual tasks at different times. This approach increases the likelihood of compliance and success.

The ultimate objective is to place a specific behavior under verbal control, so when prompted, the pet comprehends what is expected and can execute the task reliably under tranquil conditions. The owner can label this behavioral task in any way that makes sense to them. For instance, if teaching a dog to enter a kennel on command, the owner can use phrases like "kennel up" or "go to bed." Basic control tasks may include "sit/stay" or "down/stay" in a designated location, moving to a specific place on command, moving away from something (e.g., a window or door), or responding to a command to touch a body part or a click stick. The choice of tasks varies based on the desired new behavior to be established through behavior modification.

Food rewards are often effective in training dogs for new tasks. A tiered system of rewards works best, with higher-value rewards reserved for more challenging tasks and lower-value rewards for tasks the dog already knows. While food is typically the preferred reward, some pets may prefer play or a chew toy. To ensure the rewards retain their value, they should only be given to the pet when earned for performing a requested task. To prevent satiation and obesity, food rewards should be kept small, such as the size of a raisin. Novel food rewards, like peanut butter cracker bits, cheese-flavored crackers, and cereal, can be highly enticing and convenient to carry.

Maintain a schedule for follow-up, either by phone or in-person, every 7 to 10 days to assess progress, address questions, and make any necessary adjustments to keep the process on track. By inquiring about pet behavior, you can intervene early in problematic behavior and increase the likelihood of success. Breaking down tasks into manageable increments allows owners to witness progress in small steps, motivating them to continue. This benefits everyone involved.

An Example of a Behavior Modification Plan

Here's an example of a Behavior Modification Plan and what it would encompass.

REVIEWING THE TARGETED PROBLEM: Excessive Barking and Jumping on Visitors Entering the Home

SUGGESTING THE NEW DESIRED BEHAVIOR: Sitting Calmly and Quietly to Greet People Who Enter the Home

Possible Solution Components You Would Find In This Behavior Modification Plan:

- Teach the dog to sit and stay 4 to 6 feet away from the entry door.

- Train the dog to "go" to the designated location on command.

- Instruct the dog to sit and stay at the location when opening and closing the door with no one outside.

- Train the dog to sit and stay when family members enter and exit the door.

- Teach the dog to sit and stay when family members stand outside the door.

- Train the dog to sit and stay when family members approach to greet visitors.

- Initially, practice the new behavior with familiar visitors before introducing it with unfamiliar ones.

Possible Behavioral Products Suggested to Enhance Learning and Success:

- Consider using head collars such as Gentle Leader, Halti, or Snoot Loop.

- Consider utilizing a treat and train remote reward system.

Any Additional Key Elements or Recommendations for Success:

- Keep initial training sessions brief.

- Gradually phase out food rewards as each small task is mastered.

- In some cases, a tether can aid in keeping your pet in place during training.

Additional Tips for Success:

To aid in your success of implementing your new behavior modification plan, begin by focusing on holding training sessions during calm and quiet periods of time and not during events that would trigger any additional unwanted behavior.

If you find you do have to train during busy, directed times during the day or when multiple dogs are present in a home, find a way to train the dog exhibiting the problematic behavior individually, and separate them from the other dogs. It is best to train without the presence of other pets when focusing on the behavior modification training.

Lastly, you may want to consider the use of control devices, such as head collars, leashes, and harnesses, to simplify the teaching of new tasks. If you do not have experiencing working with these tools it is again highly recommended to work with a certified trainer or certified behaviorist. Having these additional tools as support during the training process can give you the additional extra control and support you need to train effectively and cut down on the time it takes to re-learn new behaviors.

Key Points to Remember when creating a Behavior Modification Plan:

When creating a Behavior Modification Plan you are looking to gain a comprehensive understanding of the problem behavior and its frequency in the canine that needs assistance. Begin by defining the desired appropriate goal/behavior and discuss strategies for managing the behavior with the owner. Then you can begin to break down the process into smaller, achievable and manageable steps. After the initial session, you will want to maintain regular follow-up with the owner to encourage them and assist them in making adjustments to their training as necessary and address any issues that arise or challenges they run into while working through each of those steps.

The Vital Role of Patience in Canine Behavior Training

Patience and persistence will be fundamental qualities for you as a successful dog trainer. Making canine behavioral changes take time, and setbacks are a natural part of the process. According to McConnell, (2002) maintaining a positive and consistent approach is key to achieving long-lasting results. So don't get discouraged. What worked for one dog doesn't always work for another. You may need to find a unique way to connect with a different dog on the same issue because, they just don't process what you're asking them to do the same way the other dog did.

It is imperative to set realistic expectations, understanding that instantaneous results should not be anticipated. Behavioral patterns are typically deeply ingrained, and altering them is a process that takes time. Consistent retraining, accompanied by redirection through positive reinforcement, is essential. This approach fosters a constructive and favorable training experience.

Embracing positive reinforcement while encouraging desired behaviors remains a key practice. Strive to maintain a positive atmosphere throughout training, steering clear of punitive measures. Patience entails the avoidance of punishment, as this can erode the trust that forms the foundation of your relationship with your dog.

Persistence and unwavering consistency in implementing rules and structure are also of paramount importance. By upholding steadfast adherence to your chosen methods, cues, and rewards, you bolster the learning process and enhance your dog's receptiveness and comprehension of the training.

Furthermore, staying informed and continually educating yourself on the latest training techniques and developments in behavioral science is essential. The industry is ever-evolving, shedding new light on the nuances of canine behavior. As long as you remain informed, you can effectively incorporate cutting-edge techniques into your training program.

In instances where professional guidance is warranted, do not hesitate to seek assistance. Diligently work toward the achievement of your behavioral goals, and if necessary, enlist the expertise of professionals who specialize in particular topics or skills. Employing positive approaches to address common behavioral issues, devising behavior modification plans, and unwaveringly applying patience and persistence in training are integral components of nurturing a well-behaved and contented canine companion.

In our upcoming chapter, we will delve into methods for broadening your dog's skill set by imparting impressive tricks and advanced obedience commands. This journey serves to further fortify the bond between you and your beloved canine companion.

Roxanne age two at Christmas.

8

CHAPTER EIGHT

Learning Advanced Commands and Tricks with Your Dog

Training your dog goes beyond the basics of sit, stay, and come. Expanding your dog's repertoire with impressive tricks and advanced obedience commands not only keeps their mind sharp but also strengthens the bond between you and your furry friend.

This chapter will guide you through the process of teaching new skills and commands as you learn how to expand and build your dog's repertoire.

Expanding You Dog's Repertoire

Broadening your dog's skill set entails introducing a diverse array of commands and behaviors to maintain an engaging and stimulating training experience. This section emphasizes instructing your dog in a wide range of skills. Once they have mastered the basics of obedience, your dog might be prepared for more advanced training. You've probably witnessed those remarkable circus dogs that can gracefully spin and bow, or the ones that steal the show in comedy acts by playing dead on command. The good news is that you can teach your furry friend these impressive tricks as well.

Benefits of Expanding Your Dogs Abilities

As you introduce new commands and engage in dog training, you naturally strengthen the bond between you and enrich your relationship. This training process fosters trust and is nurtured through the commands and tricks you impart, providing mental stimulation for your canine companion. The mental engagement, combined with your dog's focused attention during the learning process, solidifies your connection. Teaching your dog fresh commands and tricks not only stimulates their cognitive abilities but also keeps them mentally active. Expanding their skill set can enhance their overall concentration and attentiveness. Consider teaching enjoyable tricks like "Play Dead," where your dog learns to lie down on their side as if playing dead, or "Roll Over," in which you instruct them to roll over on command. For more advanced fun, explore "Spin," guiding your dog to perform a graceful circle, or "Bow," training them to elegantly lower their front legs. In addition, commencing with fundamental commands like "Leave it," which teaches your dog to promptly cease their activity and move away from a given item or temptation when commanded, and "Heel," which instructs your dog to walk calmly by your side without tugging on the leash, can offer significant benefits to your training journey.

Teaching Impressive Tricks and Commands

Mastering the art of training your dog for impressive tricks and advanced obedience commands requires patience, unwavering consistency, and a reliance on positive reinforcement. Prioritize rewarding your dog with treats, praise, or play whenever they execute the desired behavior. It's essential to employ consistent cues and reward systems to prevent any confusion. To maintain your dog's interest effectively, keep training sessions brief and engaging.

In this next session, you'll find a step-by-step guide for training specific tricks with your dog. Remember to take your time and don't get discouraged if your pup doesn't get it right away. This is a process. With consistency and positive reinforcement you will begin to see great reward from your work.

Trick 1: "Play Dead" Command

Step 1: Grab a treat.

Use a treat to lure your dog into a down position on their side.

Step 2: Add in the verbal cue, "Play Dead."

Use this as your dog starts to associate the behavior with the command.

Step 3: Repeat the steps until proficient.

Once proficient, gradually reduce the use of treats until your dog responds to the verbal command alone.

Trick 2: "Leave it" Command

Step 1: Begin with low-value items.

Choose items that your dog is less interested in.

Step 2: Show your dog a treat in your hand.

Then cover it with your thumb.

Step 3: Wait till your dog stops trying to get the treat.

When your dog stops trying to get the treat, use a release cue like "Okay" and allow them to have it.

Step 4: Increase the value of items.

Continue to practice with different objects until proficient.

Advanced Obedience Training

Advanced dog training goes beyond the fundamental basics, seeking to challenge and engage your dog both mentally and physically. Through advanced training, you can not only strengthen the bond with your dog but also enhance their obedience skills, provide a sense of purpose, and fulfill their mental and physical needs. Additionally, advanced training serves as a means to address behavioral issues and mold your dog into a well-rounded and well-behaved companion.

Before delving into advanced training, it's crucial to ensure that your dog has a solid foundation in basic obedience. They should consistently and reliably respond to fundamental commands like sit, stay, come, and heel, as these commands will serve as the cornerstone for the advanced tricks they will learn.

Commands You Can Teach Your Dog

Stay: Teach your dog to stay in one place until you release them.

Recall from a Distance: Train your dog to come to you when called from a distance.

Off-Leash Control: Work on off-leash obedience in safe and controlled environments.

Advanced Heel: Practice advanced heel work with your dog walking by your side with precision.

Advanced Obedience Techniques

Proofing involves the gradual exposure of your dog to various distractions, such as the presence of other dogs or enticing scents, while practicing advanced obedience commands.

As you witness improvements in your dog's performance, consider elevating the complexity of the commands to challenge their capabilities. If you ever find yourself reaching a plateau or desiring additional support to refine your pup's skills further, you might consider enrolling in advanced obedience classes or seeking guidance from a professional dog trainer.

Step-by-Step Guide:

Impressive Advanced Obedience Tricks

Impressive tricks and commands can be truly captivating, not only for your friends and family but also for the mental stimulation and bonding they provide to you and your dog. Teaching these remarkable tricks requires patience, consistency, and a focus on positive reinforcement. This in-depth guide will take you through the process of instructing your dog in a variety of astonishing tricks and commands that are bound to leave everyone amazed.

Trick 1: "Roll Over" Command

Step 1: Start in a Down Position

Begin with your dog in the "Down" position.

Step 2: Lure with a Treat

Hold a treat close to your dog's nose and slowly move it towards their shoulder. Your dog should follow the treat, rolling onto their side.

Step 3: Guide the Roll

As your dog follows the treat, gently guide them into a roll by moving the treat in a circular motion.

Step 4: Reward and Repeat

Once your dog completes the roll, reward them with the treat and praise. Practice this trick in short sessions to avoid frustration.

Trick 2: "Shake Hands" (Paw) Command

Step 1: Prepare Treats.

Gather small, tasty treats that your dog loves. These treats will serve as rewards during training.

Step 2: Get Your Dog's Attention.

Find a quiet, distraction-free area to start training. Call your dog's name or use a clicker if you've trained them to respond to it.

Step 3: The Basic Position.

Have your dog sit in front of you. Hold a treat in your hand, close to your dog's nose, but don't let them take it yet.

Step 4: Command and Gesture.

Say the command "Shake" or "Paw" as you extend your hand, palm open, towards your dog's paw.

Step 5: Shake Hands.

Most dogs will naturally lift their paw to reach for the treat. When your dog touches your hand with their paw, immediately reward them with the treat.

Step 6: Practice and Repeat.

Repeat the process several times. Gradually increase the duration of the paw shake before giving the treat. Always use positive reinforcement and lots of praise.

Trick 3: "Play Dead" Command

Step 1: Start in a Down Position.
Begin with your dog in the "Down" position.

Step 2: Lure with a Treat.
Hold a treat close to your dog's nose and slowly move it towards their shoulder.

Step 3: Command "Bang!"
As your dog follows the treat and starts to roll onto their side, say "Bang!" or "Play dead."

Step 4: Reward.
Once your dog is on their side, reward them with the treat.

Step 5: Practice.
Practice this trick regularly, gradually delaying the treat reward to make it more impressive.

Trick 4: "Spin" Command

Step 1: Prepare Treats.
Gather your treats.

Step 2: Command "Spin".
Stand in front of your dog. Hold a treat near their nose and say the command "Spin" while moving the treat in a circular motion in front of them.

Step 3: Guide the Spin.
As your dog follows the treat, they should spin around in a circle.

Step 4: Reward and Praise.

When your dog completes the spin, reward them with the treat and lots of praise.

Step 5: Repeat and Add a Cue.

Practice the spin command regularly, and as your dog becomes proficient, you can add a hand signal or cue without the treat.

Trick 5: "High Five" Command

Step 1: Prepare Treats.

Gather your treats.

Step 2: Command "High Five".

Have your dog sit in front of you. Hold a treat in your hand, and raise it slightly above your dog's head.

Say "High Five" as you do this.

Step 3: Reward.

When your dog raises their paw to reach for the treat, give it to them and offer praise.

Step 4: Practice.

Practice the high five command regularly, gradually using less visible cues. As your dog crawls forward, give them the treat and praise.

Step 5: Practice.

Practice the crawl command regularly, rewarding your dog for crawling longer distances.

Trick 6: "Speak" (Bark on Command)

Step 1: Prepare Treats.
Gather your treats.

Step 2: Be Silent.
Start with your dog in a quiet room with no distractions.

Step 3: Command "Speak".
Hold a treat in front of your dog but out of reach. Say the command "Speak" or "Bark" and wait for your dog to make a noise.

Step 4: Reward.
As soon as your dog barks or makes a noise, give them the treat and praise.

Step 5: Practice and Control.
Practice this command in controlled sessions. Once your dog understands the command, work on making the barking quieter or louder as needed.

Trick 7: "Crawl" Command

Step 1: Prepare Treats.
Have your treats ready.

Step 2: Command "Crawl".
Start with your dog in a "Down" position.

Step 3: Lure with a Treat.
Hold a treat close to your dog's nose and slowly move it forward along the ground.

Step 4: Reward.

Teaching your dog impressive tricks and commands can be a delightful and fulfilling experience for both you and your four-legged companion. Keep in mind the importance of using positive reinforcement, practicing patience, and maintaining short, enjoyable training sessions. With consistent effort and dedication, your dog will shine as a star performer, astonishing everyone with their newfound talents and skills.

Broadening your dog's skill set by introducing remarkable tricks, advanced obedience commands, and refining their obedience skills is a gratifying journey that strengthens your bond and enhances your dog's overall well-being. The mental stimulation and challenges provided through training contribute to a happier and more fulfilled canine companion.

In the upcoming chapter, we will delve into the significant role of mental exercise, do-it-yourself enrichment activities, and selecting the right toys and puzzles to keep your dog engaged and content.

Heidi playing fetch age three with Ryan.

9

CHAPTER NINE

Developing Activities to Engage and Stimulate the Mind

Physical exercise is important for dogs, but mental exercise is equally important. Mental stimulation helps prevent boredom, anxiety, and behavior problems while enhancing your dog's cognitive abilities. This chapter will focus on the significance of mental exercise and provide practical strategies for incorporating it into your dog's daily routine.

The Crucial Role of Mental Exercise

Mental stimulation is a crucial aspect of nurturing your dog's problem-solving skills, memory, and decision-making abilities. Prioritizing your dog's mental well-being can effectively combat boredom, discourage destructive behavior, and help alleviate anxiety and depression. Cultivating your dog's mental health is vital for their overall wellness, contributing to improved behavior and strengthening the bond between you and your four-legged companion.

Research has demonstrated that dogs engaging in mental exercises are more inclined to exhibit positive behavior. Implementing effective mental exercises to enhance your dog's cognitive abilities includes problem-solving activities, where your dog is challenged to decipher how to access a reward, often through the use of puzzle toys. Moreover, sensory stimulation, which engages their senses through activities like scent work or participation in stimulating games such as hide-and-seek, can keep their minds active and engaged. Naturally, teaching new commands and tricks also serves as an excellent method for providing mental stimulation.

DIY Enrichment Activities & Brain Games

When it comes to completing mental exercises and enrichment activities for your dog, you don't need to invest in costly toys or equipment. There are numerous creative do-it-yourself (DIY) options that can effortlessly become part of your dog's daily routine, keeping them mentally engaged and content.

For instance, you can repurpose everyday items like a Kong toy filled with your dog's preferred treats or peanut butter. Another engaging choice is a Snuffle Mat, which allows you to hide kibble or treats within the mat's fabric, encouraging your dog to use their nose to discover the goodies.

If you have a knack for DIY projects, you might consider crafting a Homemade Puzzle Toy using a muffin tin. Simply place treats or kibble in the tin's cups and cover them with tennis balls. Your dog will need to remove the balls to access the treats. Another enjoyable DIY endeavor is a Treat Bottle: cut holes in a plastic bottle, fill it with treats, and watch your dog figure out how to retrieve them.

For dogs who relish a challenge, engage in a game of Hide and Seek. Hide from your dog and encourage them to find you, using treats or a favorite toy as a reward when they succeed. You can create variations of this game by playing hide and seek with toys or family members to add variety. Alternatively, you can focus on scent work and prompt your dog to locate hidden objects or treats by following their scent trail. Start with simple searches and progressively increase the complexity to keep it enjoyable.

When choosing toys and puzzles, consider your dog's preferences and abilities. Whether its interactive toys, durable chew toys, or fetch toys, assess their preferences. Various puzzles come with varying difficulty levels, so start with easier ones and progress to more challenging ones as your dog gains confidence. Offering a variety of puzzles keeps your dog engaged and prevents boredom while helping you assess their skill level. Always prioritize safety by ensuring the toys and puzzles are free from small parts that could pose a choking hazard.

Mental exercise plays a pivotal role in your dog's overall well-being, contributing to their happiness, behavior, and cognitive development. By incorporating DIY enrichment activities, brain games, and selecting the right toys and puzzles, you can provide your canine companion with engaging mental challenges that enhance their quality of life.

In the next chapter, we will delve into adapting training methods to suit different stages of your dog's life, including puppyhood, adolescence, adulthood, and their senior years.

Nala 8 weeks old posing for the camera.

10

CHAPTER TEN

Training Across Every Stage of Life

In this chapter, we will explore the importance of adapting training methods to different life stages of dogs, from puppyhood through adolescence, adulthood, and into their senior years. Each life stage presents unique challenges and opportunities for training and behavior modification. We will also discuss how to overcome those unique challenges associated with each stage of a dog's life.

Adapting Training to Puppyhood

Puppyhood represents a crucial developmental stage in a dog's life, as effective training during this period lays the foundation for a well-behaved and self-assured adult dog. Early puppy training encompasses a vital component: socialization. Although socialization should be an ongoing process, initiating it during your puppy's early days can lead to a well-rounded and adaptable adult dog. Socialization involves exposing your puppy to various people, animals, environments, and experiences. This essential socialization window generally spans from three to fourteen weeks of age (as recommended by the American Veterinary Society of Animal Behavior, 2008).

When socializing your puppy, it's crucial to employ positive reinforcement methods to ensure that the experiences are positive and that trust is built between you and your puppy. Additionally, you can introduce basic commands as early as seven or eight weeks. Begin with fundamental commands like sit, stay, come, down, and recall. Once again, employing positive reinforcement techniques, rewards, and maintaining consistency in your training approach are vital. Keeping training sessions short and enjoyable will help maintain your puppy's attention and prevent frustration.

Furthermore, this period is an ideal time to initiate house training, often referred to as potty training. This skill is one of the initial and most essential ones to impart to your puppy.

Here are some helpful tips and a step-by-step guide to assist you in successfully house training your puppy.

Tips to House Train Your Puppy

When you embark on house training your puppy, remember that patience is of the essence. House training is a gradual process that demands time, and it's essential to acknowledge that accidents are inevitable, particularly since puppies have limited bladder control until they reach around twelve weeks of age. To initiate this process, establish a consistent routine and adhere to it diligently. Develop a feeding schedule and a potty schedule, maintaining unwavering consistency throughout. Typically, puppies need to eliminate after waking up, after eating, and before bedtime.

Continue to utilize positive reinforcement and reward your puppy with praise, treats, or playtime when they successfully eliminate outside. This approach helps them develop a positive association with going outdoors. Familiarize yourself with your puppy's cues for needing to relieve themselves, such as sniffing, circling, or whining. When you notice these signals, promptly take them outside. During the initial stages of training, closely monitor your puppy while they are indoors. You can use a leash or create a gated area to restrict their access within the house.

In the initial phases of house training, consider incorporating crate training for your puppy. Dogs are less likely to eliminate in their sleeping area, so a crate can assist them in learning to control their urges. If your puppy has an accident inside, promptly clean it up using an enzymatic cleaner to eliminate any lingering odors that might attract them back to the same spot. Avoid any form of punishment; never scold or reprimand your puppy for accidents, as this can create fear and anxiety, making the house training process more challenging.

Consistency is paramount. Ensure that all household members adhere to the same house training rules and commands to prevent confusion for your puppy. When necessary, you can adjust access to food and water, especially in the evening, to reduce the likelihood of nighttime accidents. With these strategies in place, your pup is sure to catch on in no time.

In this next section we are going to review step by step how to successfully house train your puppy in ten simple steps. Keep in mind that each puppy is unique, and the learning pace may vary. Through steadfast training, praise, and positive reinforcement, your puppy will grasp the concept of outdoor potty training and grow into a well-house trained companion.

Step-by-Step Guide:

How to House Train Your Puppy

Step 1: Preparation.
Gather necessary supplies, including a leash, treats, a crate, and enzymatic cleaner for accidents.

Step 2: Establish a Routine.
Set a consistent feeding schedule for your puppy. This will help you predict when they are likely to need to go potty.

Step 3: Frequent Potty Breaks.
Take your puppy outside frequently, especially after waking up, eating, or playing. Use a designated potty area in your yard and Wait patiently for your puppy to eliminate. Use a cue word like "Go potty" or "Do your business."

Step 4: Supervise Indoors.
When your puppy is indoors, keep them in a confined space like a small room or use a crate to prevent accidents.

Step 5: Watch for Signs.
Learn your puppy's signs of needing to go potty (e.g., sniffing, circling, whining) and take them outside immediately when you see these signs.

Step 6: Use Positive Reinforcement.
When your puppy eliminates outside, praise them enthusiastically and offer a treat as a reward.

Step 7: Prevent Nighttime Accidents.

Take your puppy out one last time before bedtime and keep them in their crate overnight.

Step 8: Consistency is Key.

Stick to your routine and be consistent with your training. Over time, your puppy will learn the appropriate place to eliminate.

Step 9: Gradual Freedom.

As your puppy becomes more reliable, gradually give them more freedom indoors under supervision.

Step 10: Be Patient.

House training can take several weeks or even months. Be patient and stay positive throughout the process.

Adapting Training to Adolescence

(6 months to 2 years)

Adolescence in dogs often comes with increased independence and occasional rebellious behavior. Adjusting your training approach during this stage is crucial for maintaining control and reinforcing obedience. Socialization remains a priority during adolescence to prevent fear and aggression issues. If you've completed basic obedience training during the puppy stage, you can now progress to more advanced commands such as "heel" and "leave it." As in all stages of training, patience is essential because adolescence can bring out stubbornness in your dog. Consistency and patience will be key to your success.

Continuing to reinforce basic obedience commands and introducing advanced ones is a crucial aspect of training adolescent dogs. Positive reinforcement remains an effective method, so using treats and praise as rewards is still recommended. It's not unusual for adolescent dogs to display sporadic obedience, but that's okay. The key is to stay patient, maintain consistency, and reward desired behaviors. With time and dedication, you will witness positive results.

Adapting Training to Adulthood

(2 years and older)

Training adult dogs typically revolves around maintaining and refining their established behavior patterns. To effectively train adult dogs, it's essential to uphold a consistent regimen of physical and mental exercise to prevent boredom. If your adult dog hasn't received basic commands or adolescent training, you may need to start there. However, if they've already mastered these foundations, you can shift your focus to more advanced skills. This stage also provides an excellent opportunity to train for specialized tasks or sports if you desire.

Adult dogs might have ingrained behaviors that require some adjustment. Behavior modification training may be necessary to address any behavioral issues as they arise. Nevertheless, adulthood brings stability and maturity to dogs, so training at this stage should primarily reinforce good behavior and address any persistent challenges. You might consider advanced training classes or specialized training, such as agility, obedience competitions, or therapy dog training. Dogs in their prime are often more receptive to learning new skills, and professional trainers or behaviorists can assist in addressing any lingering issues, like separation anxiety or aggression.

In the meantime, it's crucial to maintain a regular exercise routine and engage your dog in mentally stimulating activities to prevent boredom and curb unwanted behaviors.

Training for Senior Dogs

As dogs transition into their senior years, their training requirements evolve due to the physical and cognitive changes associated with aging. Training should aim to maintain their quality of life and address age-related challenges. It's crucial to adapt your approach during this phase by using simpler cues and keeping training sessions shorter to accommodate their changing needs. Patience becomes even more critical, and older dogs may need additional time to respond to commands. Acknowledge their physical limitations and adjust your expectations accordingly. If needed, modify activities and exercises to align with their capabilities.

Canine Health and Well-being

Prior to commencing any training regimen, it is vital to ensure that your dog is in good health and ready for training. This commences with a thorough veterinary examination to clear them for training activities. The examination addresses not only current health concerns but also ensures that your dog is up to date on vaccinations before engaging in public activities. Being in public without proper vaccinations can pose health risks and financial burdens for owners.

Once your dog has received the veterinarian's clearance, it is wise to maintain their well-being through the provision of quality nutrition, regular exercise, and necessary medications, such as flea and tick prevention or any prescribed medication. As training activities increase, you may need to adjust their diet to meet their evolving nutritional needs. Senior dogs, in particular, may require special dietary adaptations, just as they may need tailored adjustments in their training program.

Assessing the cognitive health of senior dogs is important. If signs of cognitive decline are evident, incorporating brain games and puzzles can help keep their minds active. Furthermore, be mindful of age-related health issues, such as arthritis or vision problems, and adapt training techniques accordingly.

A holistic approach to your dog's health encompasses maintaining a healthy, active lifestyle, a nutritious diet, essential vitamins, and the proper balance of exercise and mental stimulation. Social interaction is key for dogs, helping reduce anxiety and aggression. Regular veterinary check-ups, dental care, grooming, and emotional well-being through love and attention all play essential roles in your dog's overall health.

Balanced nutrition is crucial for your dog's well-being, and your veterinarian can guide you in choosing the best diet based on your dog's age, size, and activity level. Prioritize high-quality dog food with specific protein sources and essential nutrients, with precise portion measurements to prevent overfeeding.

Adding supplements to your dog's diet, such as fish oil, glucosamine and chondroitin, or multivitamins, should be done under professional guidance. Consult with your veterinarian before introducing any supplements to ensure they meet your dog's health and dietary needs.

Regular check-ups with your veterinarian help monitor your dog's overall health, early issue detection, and vaccinations, as well as preventative treatments such as flea and tick control and heartworm prevention.

Oral health should not be overlooked, as regular teeth cleaning and dental check-ups can prevent dental issues that may lead to other health problems. Maintaining a healthy weight is essential, as obesity can lead to various health concerns, including joint problems and diabetes.

Keeping fleas, ticks, and internal parasites at bay is critical for your dog's health. Consult your veterinarian for appropriate preventive measures based on your dog's lifestyle and risk factors.

Maintaining proper hygiene practices, including ear cleaning and nail trimming, can help prevent infections and skin problems.

Don't forget the importance of emotional care, providing love, attention, and a comfortable environment to reduce stress and anxiety.

Taking a holistic approach to your dog's health, including healthy living, a balanced diet, supplements when necessary, and regular veterinary care, contributes to a longer and happier life for your furry companion. Consult with your veterinarian for personalized advice regarding your dog's specific health needs.

Overcoming Unique Challenges at Each Stage

Every stage of life brings unique challenges when it comes to training and behavior modification. Recognizing these challenges enables you to tailor your training approach for success. Nevertheless, it's important to acknowledge that breed-specific challenges can also play a significant role, as we will explore in the following section.

Breed Specific Challenges

In addition to the primary life stages, specific breed-related challenges can arise due to the distinct characteristics and tendencies of each breed. Tailoring your training approach to accommodate these breed-specific traits is crucial. It's essential to thoroughly research your dog's breed traits and adjust your training methods to meet their specific needs. Consider incorporating activities and exercises that align with their natural instincts.

Consistency is key in your training methods and expectations, as dogs thrive on routine and clear boundaries. Throughout your dog's life, positive reinforcement remains a powerful motivator for cooperation and helps strengthen the bond between you and your dog.

If you encounter difficulties or challenging behaviors, don't hesitate to seek the guidance of a certified dog trainer or behaviorist who can provide customized solutions to address your specific concerns [Arden and Adams, 2016].

Adapting your training methods to suit various life stages, from puppyhood to the senior years, is essential for nurturing a well-adjusted and well-behaved canine companion. Each stage offers its unique challenges and training opportunities. By maintaining consistency, embracing positive reinforcement, and seeking professional assistance when needed, you can provide the best possible training experience for your dog throughout their entire life.

Riley age three during his photo shoot.

CHAPTER ELEVEN

Creating a Harmonious Home with Multiples

In this chapter, we will delve into the complexities of training and managing multiple dogs while addressing interpersonal conflicts among them. Whether you are part of a multi-dog household or contemplating the addition of a new pet, comprehending the dynamics and implementing established strategies is essential for fostering harmony and nurturing positive relationships among your four-legged companions.

Intricacies of Training Multiple Dogs

Training multiple dogs can offer both gratification and complexity, as it necessitates catering to individual needs while fostering a sense of unity within the group. When conducting group training sessions, it's advisable to allocate separate training periods for each dog to address their distinct requirements and commands. Creating a tranquil, distraction-free environment is essential for enhancing concentration.

Within a group setting, it's pivotal to emphasize socialization and cooperative behavior while employing positive reinforcement techniques to promote teamwork. For dogs unaccustomed to this environment, aiding their adaptation is imperative. Consistently maintaining rules and routines for all dogs is crucial to minimize confusion, and the consistent rewarding of desired behaviors reinforces the training. Providing individualized attention, exercise, and mental stimulation to each dog can prevent jealousy or competition and teach them to tolerate separation, reducing stress when they are apart.

Introducing a new pet into a multi-dog household necessitates thoughtful planning and a gradual approach. Initiate the introduction of the new pet and resident dogs in a neutral territory, such as a park. Begin with brief, supervised interactions and gradually extend their time together. Use positive reinforcement to reward calm and friendly behaviors with treats and praise. Address any signs of tension or aggression promptly and seek professional assistance if necessary. Engaging both new and resident dogs in parallel activities during the integration process, like walks, playtime, and training sessions, can be beneficial. Initially, provide separate spaces for eating, sleeping, and relaxation, and gradually allow shared spaces as their comfort and compatibility increase. Always supervise interactions until you are confident in their ability to coexist peacefully.

Interpersonal conflicts among dogs are not uncommon and can occur in various scenarios. These conflicts may stem from resource guarding, territorial behavior, fear, anxiety, or a lack of socialization. Dogs communicate through body language, vocalizations, and signals, and misunderstandings or ineffective communication can lead to conflicts.

Preventing these conflicts is the most effective approach to ensuring the safety and well-being of all the dogs involved. It's essential to comprehend the underlying causes of conflicts and use positive reinforcement to encourage desirable behaviors. Training dogs to respond to commands and cues can enhance their obedience and impulse control, reducing the likelihood of conflicts. If conflicts persist, seeking the assistance of a professional dog trainer or behaviorist to create a behavior modification plan is advisable. This plan may include desensitization, counter-conditioning, and teaching alternative behaviors.

In the meantime, managing resources by feeding dogs separately, providing multiple water and food bowls, and removing high-value items when conflicts arise can be helpful. Use body language and vocal cues to intervene when conflicts occur, diverting attention or separating dogs temporarily to prevent escalation. In cases of serious or persistent conflicts, professional guidance and interventions are recommended to address the issues effectively and ensure the safety of all the dogs involved.

Ginger at 6 months old and member of the poodle crew.

12

CHAPTER TWELVE

Reflecting on Your Training Journey with Your Canine

In this chapter, we will explore the importance of reflecting on your training journey with your canine companion. We will delve into the lifelong benefits of positive reinforcement training and discuss the value of continuing education and advanced training for both you and your dog.

Revisiting Your Experiences

Taking the time for self-reflection during your dog training journey is a valuable practice that enables you to evaluate your progress, revel in achievements, and pinpoint areas for enhancement. Moreover, it deepens the connection between you and your furry companion. As you embark on this introspective journey, pause to marvel at the strides you and your dog have made since the inception of your training voyage. Acknowledge the commands your dog has mastered and the behavioral improvements they've demonstrated. Rejoice in your accomplishments by recalling specific training milestones and instances when your dog surpassed your expectations. Pay homage to and reinforce these triumphs, as they cultivate positivity throughout your training expedition.

Beyond celebrating your victories, take time to reflect on the hurdles you've encountered along the way. Contemplate any setbacks or behaviors that still require attention. Recognizing these challenges is the first step toward managing them effectively.

Reflect on the learning moments and the insights you've gained as both a trainer and a dog owner. Ponder the training techniques and methods that have proven most effective for your dog, as well as those that may warrant adjustments. Deliberate on the strengthening bond and rapport you've developed with your dog through training. Evaluate how your communication has improved and how well you understand each other. Adaptability is a pivotal aspect of successful training. Assess your consistency as a trainer, ensuring that you consistently follow through with commands and reinforce good behavior, as consistency is a cornerstone of effective training.

Contemplate your patience and the understanding that dogs progress at varying rates. Patience is paramount for maintaining a positive training atmosphere. Scrutinize your training environment and its suitability for learning, taking into account the presence of minimal distractions and abundant positive reinforcement.

Revisit your initial training goals from the outset of your journey and determine whether they have evolved over time. Modify your objectives as necessary to align with your dog's growth and your training aspirations. Envision your next steps in the training expedition. What new commands or behaviors do you wish to explore with your dog? Are you interested in pursuing advanced training or engaging in canine sports? Reflect on the resources and support you've tapped into during your training odyssey, such as guidance from trainers, books, online courses, or fellow dog owners. Assess their effectiveness and decide if you require additional assistance.

When considering your dog's health and well-being, contemplate their overall physical and mental requirements. Ensure that these needs are being met through exercise, mental stimulation, and proper care.

Acknowledge that learning is an ongoing process and contemplate how you can further expand your knowledge and skills in dog training and behavior. Reflect on the joy and fulfillment you've experienced throughout your training expedition. Always remember that training should be a positive and enjoyable journey for both you and your dog. Express gratitude for the privilege of sharing your life with a canine companion and the growth and enrichment your dog has brought into your life. Reflecting on your training journey empowers you to appreciate the progress achieved, recommit to your training objectives, and fortify the bond with your dog. It's an enduring and rewarding process that contributes to a harmonious relationship with your four-legged friend.

The Lifelong Benefits of Positive Reinforcement

Positive reinforcement training is a fundamental pillar of successful dog training, offering enduring advantages for your furry companion. These benefits encompass improved communication, heightened self-assurance, and enhanced behavior, a deeper bond between you and your dog, reduced stress, and more. The primary aim of positive reinforcement is to bolster the connection between you and your dog, forging a partnership founded on trust and mutual regard. This training approach steers clear of fear-based methods and cultivates a more secure and emotionally resilient dog by consistently rewarding desired behaviors to refine their conduct.

As you advance your knowledge and progress in your training, both you and your dog assume pivotal roles in nurturing a healthy, rewarding, and harmonious relationship. Moving forward in your training expedition will introduce fresh challenges and opportunities for personal and canine growth.

Here's a guide on how to pursue continuing education and advance your career in dog training.

Advancing Your Expertise in Dog Training:
A Lifelong Journey

Dog training is a dynamic and evolving field, one that requires continuous learning and adaptation to provide the best care for our four-legged companions. The process of educating and shaping a dog's behavior goes far beyond teaching basic commands. It is about creating a fulfilling and harmonious relationship between humans and their canine friends. To embark on this lifelong journey and become a successful dog trainer, one must be committed to ongoing education and self-improvement.

Advanced Training Classes and Workshops

The first step in advancing your expertise in dog training is to seek out advanced training classes and workshops. These programs are available in your local area and cover a wide range of topics, including advanced obedience, agility, rally, canine sports, and specialized skills. Participating in these courses allows you to expand your skill set and develop a deeper understanding of advanced training techniques.

Online Courses and Webinars

In addition to local classes, explore online courses and webinars offered by reputable dog trainers and behaviorists. Many organizations and professionals provide these online learning opportunities, making it convenient to access a wealth of knowledge. These resources cover various aspects of dog training and behavior, providing a flexible and accessible way to broaden your expertise.

Certification Programs

Consider enrolling in a dog training certification program. Earning a certification not only validates your expertise but also enhances your credibility as a dog trainer. Certification signifies your dedication to the profession and demonstrates your commitment to maintaining a high standard of training. It is a crucial step in establishing yourself as a professional in the field.

Seminars and Conferences

Attending seminars, workshops, and conferences related to dog training and behavior is another valuable means of advancing your knowledge. These events often feature leading experts who share their knowledge and insights. Participating in these gatherings allows you to learn from the best in the industry, stay updated on the latest trends, and gain practical skills that you can apply to your training techniques.

Continuous Reading and Research

To stay at the forefront of the field, continuously read books, articles, and research papers on dog training, behavior, and canine psychology. Understanding the latest developments and research findings is essential for refining your skills and staying informed about the evolving science of dog behavior.

Networking with Fellow Enthusiasts

Connecting with fellow dog owners and trainers through local dog clubs, online forums, and social media groups can be a valuable source of support, advice, and new perspectives. Networking allows you to share experiences, exchange ideas, and gain insights from others who share your passion for canine training.

Seeking Mentorship

One of the most effective ways to accelerate your growth as a dog trainer is to seek mentorship from experienced trainers or behaviorists. Learning from someone with more expertise can provide valuable guidance, feedback, and real-world insights that you may not gain through formal education alone. Mentorship is a unique opportunity to benefit from the wisdom of those who have been in the field for many years.

Volunteering at Animal Shelters

Consider volunteering at animal shelters or rescue organizations. This hands-on experience enables you to work with a variety of dogs and further develop your training skills. It also allows you to make a positive impact on the lives of shelter dogs by helping them become more adoptable through training.

Continuing Education for Certified Trainers

If you are a certified dog trainer, ensure that you fulfill continuing education requirements to maintain your certification. Keeping your knowledge and skills up-to-date is crucial for preserving your professional credentials and providing the best possible training to your clients and their dogs.

In conclusion, becoming a successful dog trainer is a journey of lifelong learning and growth. Seek out advanced training opportunities, embrace certification programs, attend seminars and conferences, read extensively, network with fellow enthusiasts, and seek mentorship. Combine these efforts with hands-on experience through volunteering at shelters. By following these steps, you will continue to advance your expertise in dog training, providing the highest level of care and training for your beloved canine companions. The bond between humans and dogs deepens through effective training, creating a fulfilling and harmonious relationship that lasts a lifetime.

Advancing the Canine Connection: A Lifelong Journey

The bond between humans and dogs is a profound and enduring one. As responsible pet owners, we strive to provide our canine companions with the best possible life, filled with love, care, and enrichment. A key aspect of this commitment is the ongoing training and development of our dogs. Training is not a one-time event but a lifelong journey that strengthens our connection with our furry friends.

Advanced Training and Skills Development

To foster the intellectual and emotional growth of your dog, consider enrolling them in advanced obedience classes. These classes reinforce and expand their obedience skills, ensuring that they remain well-behaved and responsive. Such classes are a vital component of building a strong foundation for your dog's training journey as well as creating a bond between you and your dog.

Furthermore, take a moment to explore the world of canine sports, including activities like agility, fly ball, obedience trials, and scent work. These sports not only provide mental and physical stimulation but also strengthen the bond between you and your dog as well. Engaging in these sports is a fantastic way to deepen your connection while promoting overall well-being.

For those with dogs that exhibit a unique aptitude, consider specialized training in roles such as search and rescue, therapy dog work, or service dog tasks. These skills are invaluable, as they enable your dog to contribute to society while strengthening your bond through shared purpose.

Teaching your dog advanced tricks and commands can be both mentally enriching and entertaining. This practice challenges their cognitive abilities and deepens their understanding of your cues, leading to a more harmonious and connected partnership.

Canine freestyle is a creative and fun way to bond with your dog through movement and music. This activity combines obedience, dance, and choreography, offering a unique opportunity to express your creativity and shared enjoyment.

Competitions and Socialization

For those with competitive spirits, consider entering your dog into obedience trials, agility competitions, or other dog sports events. Participation in such events not only provides a platform for showcasing your dog's talents but also fosters a sense of achievement and camaraderie.

Continuing to socialize your dog throughout their life is crucial for ensuring they remain well-adjusted and comfortable in various environments. Exposure to different people, animals, and situations enhances their adaptability and strengthens their social skills.

Physical and Mental Well-being

Physical activity is a vital component of your dog's well-being. Regular exercise not only keeps them in good physical shape but also contributes to their mental health. Daily walks, runs, and playtime in the park are essential for your dog's overall happiness and mental stimulation.

Incorporate puzzle toys and brain games into your dog's routine. These activities engage their cognitive abilities and provide hours of entertainment. A mentally stimulated dog is a contented and well-rounded companion.

Health Maintenance and Positive Reinforcement

Regular vet checkups are crucial to monitor your dog's health as they age. Preventive care and early intervention can help identify and address any physical or behavioral changes promptly.

Advanced training should always be grounded in positive reinforcement techniques that prioritize your dog's well-being and enjoyment. Continuous adjustment of your training methods to align with your dog's unique needs and capabilities ensures a positive and fruitful training journey.

In conclusion, the journey of training and growing alongside your dog is a lifelong commitment filled with boundless opportunities for connection, enrichment, and shared accomplishments. Embrace advanced training, sports, and skills development to keep your dog's mind and body engaged. Cherish the shared experiences, and prioritize their well-being through regular exercise and mental stimulation. Your commitment to positive reinforcement and ongoing education will not only improve your dog's behavior but also strengthen the deep bond and shared understanding between you. Celebrate your progress, reinforce positive behaviors, and remain dedicated to continuous learning as you and your dog embark on a rewarding and harmonious life-long journey together.

Welcome Harry Winston! Our newest member to the poodle crew.

CHAPTER THIRTEEN

Celebrating Stories of Success

In this final chapter, we will celebrate the success stories of dog owners who have embarked on the journey of training and nurturing their canine companions. We will explore the importance of fostering a positive community of dog owners and share the vision of a bright future with your well-trained and happy canine companion.

Celebrating Success Stories with Dogs that Experienced Positive Reinforcement Training

The journey of dog training is filled with countless success stories. These stories serve as a testament to the power of positive reinforcement, patience, and the strong bond between humans and their canine companions. Here are a few remarkable success stories:

From Fear to Confidence

Meet Bella, a rescued dog who was once afraid of strangers due to her past experiences. Through positive reinforcement training and socialization, Bella transformed into a confident and friendly dog who loves meeting new people [McConnell, 2002].

Overcoming Aggression

Jake, a rescue dog, had a history of aggression toward other dogs. His owner, Sarah, worked with a professional trainer to address his behavior using positive reinforcement techniques. Today, Jake enjoys peaceful walks in the park and even has canine friends he plays with (Herron et al., 2009).

Bonding through Training

Emily adopted Max, a high-energy border collie. They embarked on a journey of obedience training and agility courses, strengthening their bond and achieving impressive agility competition success (Arden and Adams, 2016).

Building Confidence in Shy Dogs

Daisy, a shy rescue dog, was terrified of loud noises and new environments. Her owner, John, used desensitization and positive reinforcement to build her confidence. Now, Daisy happily accompanies John on hikes and has become a therapy dog for children with anxiety (Overall, 2013).

From Shy Rescue to Confident Companion

Dog: Bailey, a Shetland sheepdog mix

Owner: Sarah

Background: Bailey was rescued from a shelter and had a history of extreme shyness and fearfulness. He cowered and trembled around people and other dogs, making it challenging for Sarah to provide him with a fulfilling life.

Positive Reinforcement Journey: Sarah embarked on a journey to help Bailey overcome his fears using positive reinforcement training techniques. She introduced Bailey to treats he loved, such as small bits of chicken, to create positive associations with her presence. She used clicker training to mark and reward small moments of bravery and curiosity. Slowly, Sarah exposed Bailey to controlled, positive experiences with other dogs and people in a safe and controlled environment. Through patience, consistency, and positive reinforcement, Bailey's confidence began to grow.

Result: Over time, Bailey transformed from a shy and fearful dog into a confident and outgoing companion. He now eagerly approaches people and enjoys playing with other dogs at the park. Positive reinforcement training helped him build trust in humans and the world around him.

Overcoming Aggression with Love and Positive Reinforcement

Dog: Duke, a Pit Bull Terrier

Owner: Alex

Background: Duke exhibited aggression towards strangers and had a history of fear-based aggression. His owner, Alex, was committed to addressing this issue without resorting to punitive methods.

Positive Reinforcement Journey: Alex turned to positive reinforcement training and consulted with a certified dog trainer. She used treats and praise to reward Duke for calm and non-aggressive behavior. She implemented a "look at me" command to redirect Duke's attention from potential triggers. She gradually exposed Duke to controlled situations where he could interact positively with strangers, always rewarding calm behavior. Consistent training sessions and ongoing reinforcement were essential to Duke's progress.

Result: Through positive reinforcement training and consistent effort, Duke's aggression towards strangers significantly decreased. He learned to associate strangers with positive experiences, leading to a more relaxed and sociable demeanor. Duke and Alex can now enjoy walks and outings with fewer anxiety-driven reactions.

These real-life success stories demonstrate how positive reinforcement training can transform dogs with behavioral challenges into confident, well-adjusted companions. Patience, consistency, and a focus on positive associations are key elements to these success stories.

Molly's Confidence Boost

Background: Molly, a Border collie mix, was rescued from an abusive situation. She was extremely timid and fearful of people and other dogs.

Approach: Molly's owner, Sarah, decided to use positive reinforcement techniques to help build Molly's confidence. She used treats, praise, and clicker training to reward Molly for small steps towards socialization.

Result: Over time, Molly started to associate positive experiences with interactions. She learned to trust Sarah and began to approach new people and dogs with curiosity rather than fear. Molly's transformation from a fearful dog to a confident and social companion was truly remarkable.

Rocky's Recall Success

Background: Rocky, a high-energy Golden Retriever, had a tendency to dash off when off-leash, making it challenging for his owner, Mark, to trust him during outdoor activities.

Approach: Mark decided to focus on recall training using positive reinforcement. He used high-value treats and enthusiastic praise every time Rocky returned promptly when called.

Result: Through consistent positive reinforcement, Rocky's recall improved dramatically. He became reliable off-leash, allowing Mark to enjoy outdoor adventures with confidence and peace of mind.

Overcoming Separation Anxiety

Background: Max, a Labrador mix, struggled with severe separation anxiety. He would bark, whine, and engage in destructive behavior whenever his owner, Lisa, left the house.

Approach: Lisa sought the help of a certified positive reinforcement trainer. They implemented a gradual desensitization program, using treats and rewards to create positive associations with alone time.

Result: Over several weeks of patient training, Max's anxiety reduced significantly. He learned to associate being alone with positive experiences, and his destructive behaviors ceased. Max and Lisa were able to enjoy a harmonious relationship without the stress of separation anxiety.

Lily's Aggression Turnaround

Background: Lily, a Pit Bull mix, exhibited aggression towards other dogs due to fear and insecurity.

Approach: Lily's owner, Mike, enrolled in a positive reinforcement-based group training class. The trainer used careful desensitization techniques and rewarded Lily for calm behavior around other dogs.

Result: Through consistent positive reinforcement and controlled exposure to other dogs, Lily's confidence grew. She learned that interactions with other dogs could be positive and enjoyable. Over time, Lily's aggression diminished, and she became more relaxed in social situations.

These real-life tales of triumph illustrate the effectiveness of positive reinforcement training in helping typical dogs conquer diverse behavioral challenges and enhancing the quality of life for both dogs and their owners. It's crucial to bear in mind that every dog is one of a kind, and outcomes may differ. Seeking advice from a certified positive reinforcement trainer or behaviorist can offer customized guidance for your particular circumstances.

How to Become a Part of Your Local Dog Training Community

A positive community of dog owners plays a vital role in promoting responsible pet ownership, sharing knowledge, and providing support. This is a great place to share your training journey and success stories with other dog owners.

It is a great place where you can offer insight and advice based on your experiences. Here they offer various training classes available for pet owners to attend with their dogs, catering to different needs and skill levels.

Here are some different types of classes available to you that you may find interesting and may also be available in you city or town:

Puppy Socialization Classes: These classes are designed for young puppies to help them develop important social skills and behaviors. They focus on basic obedience and socialization with other dogs and people.

Basic Obedience Classes: These classes cover fundamental commands such as sit, stay, come, and leash walking. They are suitable for puppies and adult dogs who need to learn or reinforce basic manners.

Advanced Obedience Classes: For dogs that have mastered the basics, advanced classes offer more challenging commands, off-leash training, and increased focus on precision and reliability.

Agility Classes: Agility training involves guiding your dog through a timed obstacle course. It's not only a great physical workout but also mentally stimulating for your dog.

Canine Good Citizen (CGC) Classes: The CGC program teaches dogs to be well-behaved and responsible members of their communities. Dogs who pass the CGC test often have access to more public places.

Therapy Dog Training: These classes prepare dogs to become therapy animals that provide comfort and support in hospitals, nursing homes, and other settings.

Service Dog Training: Designed for dogs that will assist individuals with disabilities, service dog training covers specific tasks and behaviors necessary to help their handlers.

Behavior Modification Classes: These classes are tailored to address specific behavioral issues such as aggression, anxiety, or fearfulness. They often involve one-on-one instruction with a professional behaviorist.

Trick Training Classes: Trick training is a fun way to bond with your dog and teach those entertaining tricks and commands beyond the basics.

Scent Detection Classes: Dogs in these classes learn to use their keen sense of smell to locate and identify specific scents. It's a great activity for scent hounds and working breeds.

Rally Obedience Classes: Rally obedience combines elements of traditional obedience and agility. Dogs follow a course with various signs that instruct them on different tasks.

Fly ball Classes: Fly ball is a high-energy team sport where dogs race over hurdles to trigger a spring-loaded box that releases a tennis ball.

Hunting or Retrieving Classes: These classes are ideal for breeds with a natural hunting or retrieving instinct. Dogs learn to work with their owners in hunting or retrieving activities.

Herding Classes: Breeds with herding instincts can learn to herd livestock or participate in herding trials.

Online Training Classes: In recent years, many trainers have started offering online training classes, allowing pet owners to learn and practice from the comfort of their homes.

When selecting a training class for your dog, consider your dog's age, breed, temperament, and your specific goals. You may also want to consider participating in group training classes or group workshops in your community that give you the ability to interact with other fellow dog owners, give you a chance to exchange ideas and build new connections. If you still have questions, reach out to a qualified trainer or behaviorist in your area and they may have additional information specific to your location.

How Can I Support My Local Shelter and Animal Rescues?

Once you've pinpointed the local shelters and rescue organizations in your vicinity, it's advisable to explore their websites, initiate direct contact, or pay them a visit to familiarize yourself with their adoption procedures, available dogs, and adoption fees. Moreover, consider a personal visit to these shelters to meet the dogs in person, helping you find the perfect match for your family and lifestyle.

Another meaningful way to contribute is by volunteering at a local shelter or rescue organization. This not only benefits a dog in need but also brings a sense of fulfillment through giving and assisting others. Collaborating with like-minded individuals to raise awareness about adoption and responsible pet ownership, as noted by Arhant et al., (2010) can yield remarkable results.

In case you encounter challenges while locating shelters or rescues in your area, it might be worthwhile to reach out to your local animal control services department or regional animal welfare organizations dedicated to animal well-being. They may possess valuable information regarding nearby shelters and rescues, offering guidance to set you in the right direction.

What Online Community Resources are Available for the Training Community?

Over the years, there has been a surge in the availability of online community resources within the dog training community. If you are seeking information or additional resources related to dog training in your community, you can effectively utilize search engines such as Google by employing specific keywords like "dog shelters near me" or "dog rescues in [your city/region]." This approach will yield a comprehensive list of local organizations.

Pet adoption websites serve as valuable resources, depending on the type of information you are seeking. Websites like Petfinder, Adopt-a-Pet, and RescueMe.org enable you to search for adoptable dogs based on your location.

The influence of social media has grown significantly in recent years, with many shelters and rescue organizations now maintaining an online presence on platforms like Facebook, Instagram, and Twitter. You can search for these organizations in your area and follow their pages to stay updated on available dogs.

Online forums dedicated to positive dog training have also gained prominence. According to Rooney and Cowan (2011), these forums offer a plethora of resources for engaging in community discussions online. They provide a platform for seeking advice and actively participating in a supportive online community focused on training.

In summary, the internet offers a wealth of resources for individuals seeking information and community engagement in the field of dog training, making it easier than ever to connect with local organizations and like-minded individuals.

Educational Dog Events: Unleashing Knowledge for Canine Enthusiasts

Dogs have been our faithful companions for centuries, but to truly appreciate and care for our four-legged friends, we must continuously expand our understanding of them. Educational events about dogs serve as a powerful platform for pet owners and dog enthusiasts to delve into the realms of canine behavior, training, health, and responsible pet ownership. These events offer a blend of enlightenment and enjoyment while creating opportunities for networking and connecting with fellow dog lovers. In this essay, we will explore a wide array of educational dog events, highlighting the benefits and significance of each.

Dog Training Workshops: The Path to Canine Excellence

Effective training is essential for a well-behaved and harmonious relationship with our dogs. Dog Training Workshops are a gateway to mastering the art of canine training. Led by experienced educators and trainers, these workshops cover a spectrum of training aspects, from basic obedience to advanced skills. Participants not only gain theoretical knowledge but also engage in hands-on training techniques, learning from the best in the field. The bond between dogs and their owners deepens as they discover the magic of trust and cooperation.

Large Pet Expos: A Grand Canine Knowledge Fair

Large pet expos are grand knowledge fairs for pet enthusiasts, featuring educational booths, captivating demonstrations, and expert speakers. These events offer a vast spectrum of information, encompassing not only dogs but also various other pets. Attendees can interact with experts, ask questions, and stay updated on the latest developments in the pet industry. Moreover, these expos provide a delightful environment for networking with like-minded individuals who share a passion for our four-legged companions.

Canine Behavior Seminars: Decoding Dog Language

Understanding the intricacies of canine behavior is crucial for both training and responsible pet ownership. Canine Behavior Seminars are designed to dive deep into the world of dog behavior. Topics such as interpreting body language, addressing fear and aggression, and managing anxiety in dogs are thoroughly explored. These seminars provide a comprehensive understanding of how dogs communicate and respond to stimuli, thus fostering healthier and more harmonious relationships between dogs and their owners.

Communication Workshops: Strengthening the Human-Canine Bond

Effective communication is the foundation of a strong and mutually fulfilling human-canine bond. Communication Workshops focus on teaching participants how to communicate effectively with their dogs, emphasizing the interpretation of body language and the use of positive reinforcement training methods. These workshops ensure that the lines of communication between pet and owner remain open, respectful, and filled with trust.

Puppy Socialization Classes: Nurturing Well-Rounded Canines

Community groups often host Puppy Socialization Classes, offering a safe and controlled environment for puppies to interact with other dogs and people. These classes play a pivotal role in helping puppies develop crucial social skills. Through positive interactions, they gain confidence and learn how to navigate various social settings, setting the stage for well-rounded development.

Breed-Specific Events: Celebrating Canine Diversity

Breed-specific clubs frequently organize educational events that focus on a particular breed's history, characteristics, and care requirements. These events celebrate the rich diversity of dog breeds and provide insights into their unique needs. The American Kennel Club (AKC) hosts events across the United States, offering enthusiasts the opportunity to explore and learn about various breeds.

Canine Health and Wellness Fairs: A Holistic Approach

Canine Health and Wellness Fairs are held at various locations in the United States during specific times of the year. These events provide a holistic approach to dog care, covering topics such as nutrition, vaccinations, dental care, and preventive healthcare. Veterinarians and experts are often on hand to answer questions and provide guidance on keeping dogs healthy and happy.

Agility and Obedience Trials: Witnessing Canine Excellence

Agility and Obedience Trials are a source of fascination for dog enthusiasts. Attending these competitions allows individuals to witness skilled trainers and dogs in action. Observing these trials provides insights into training techniques and how dogs respond to commands. Furthermore, these events often feature demonstrations of dog sports like fly ball, dock diving, and herding trials, inspiring dog owners to explore new activities with their canine companions.

Presentations on Therapy and Service Dogs: Life-Changing Roles

For those interested in the remarkable roles of therapy and service dogs, presentations offer a window into the training and impact of these incredible canines. These dogs provide invaluable support in various settings, from healthcare facilities to assisting individuals with disabilities.

Additional Health and Wellness Events: Caring Holistically

Canine Nutrition Workshops delve into the significance of proper nutrition for a dog's health and well-being. Discussions encompass commercial diets, raw feeding, and homemade diets, offering insights into the best practices for nourishing our canine companions.

Pet First Aid and CPR Classes teach essential first aid and CPR techniques for dogs, equipping participants with the skills to act swiftly in case of emergencies. These skills can be invaluable in potentially life-threatening situations.

Canine Science and Research Lectures offer a window into the latest scientific discoveries and research related to dogs' behavior, cognition, and genetics, further enhancing our understanding of these amazing animals.

Dog Owner Education Programs provide comprehensive coverage of everything from basic dog care to advanced training techniques. These programs are typically offered by professional trainers or veterinarians, ensuring that pet owners have access to the best guidance and knowledge.

A World of Canine Knowledge Awaits

To discover educational events about dogs in your area, you can begin by checking with local dog training schools, veterinary clinics, pet stores, breed clubs, and animal shelters. These organizations often host or can guide you to events that align with your interests. Additionally, you can search online event listings and social media platforms for announcements and schedules of upcoming dog-related educational events and seminars.

Educational dog events open doors to a world of knowledge and understanding, celebrating the bond between humans and canines. These events offer the opportunity to connect with like-minded individuals, fostering a community of dog enthusiasts who are dedicated to enhancing the lives of their furry companions. As we continue to explore and learn about the world of dogs, we strengthen our commitment to responsible pet ownership and create more enriching relationships with our beloved pets.

The Bright Future of Your Well-Trained & Happy Canine Companion

The future for your well-trained and happy canine companion is a canvas filled with endless possibilities. As a responsible dog owner, you've invested time and effort into training and nurturing your furry friend, and now it's time to reap the rewards. Your future with your dog holds the promise of exciting adventures, bonding experiences, and cherished memories.

Exploring New Adventures

Your well-trained and happy dog is the perfect partner for exploring new adventures, fostering a deeper connection, and enhancing both physical and mental well-being. Dogs are natural companions for outdoor activities and can make any adventure memorable. Here are some exhilarating adventures to consider:

Hiking: Explore nature trails, forests, and mountains with your dog. Make sure to choose dog-friendly trails and keep your dog on a leash where required. Bring essentials like water, a leash, waste bags, and snacks for both you and your furry friend.

Camping: Camping trips allow you and your dog to disconnect from the hustle and bustle of daily life. Ensure you're staying at a dog-friendly campground, and remember to pack dog food, bedding, and any necessary camping gear for your pup.

Beach Days: Many dogs love the water. Take your dog to a dog-friendly beach for a day of swimming and playing in the sand. Be mindful of beach regulations and bring fresh water for hydration.

Kayaking or Canoeing: If you enjoy water sports, consider bringing your dog along for a kayaking or canoeing adventure. Ensure your dog is comfortable with water and has a life jacket for safety.

Biking: Some dogs can keep up with your biking adventures. Invest in a dog bike leash or trailer to safely take your pup along for the ride.

Road Trips: Plan dog-friendly road trips to explore new destinations together. Research pet-friendly hotels and accommodations in advance, and don't forget to secure your dog safely in the car.

Agility Courses: Enroll in agility classes or find a local dog park with agility equipment. These courses provide mental and physical stimulation for your dog while strengthening your bond.

Fly ball: Try your hand at fly ball, a relay race for dogs, which combines speed and agility. It's a fun and competitive way to bond with your pup.

Geocaching: Geocaching is like a treasure hunt using GPS coordinates. Many geocaches are dog-friendly and provide an opportunity for exploration.

Dog-Friendly Wineries or Breweries: Some wineries and breweries allow dogs on their patios. Enjoy a relaxing afternoon while your dog socializes with other patrons.

Sledding or Skijoring: In colder climates, consider trying sledding or skijoring with your dog. These activities are especially enjoyable for Northern breeds.

Trail Running: If you're a runner, bring your dog along for trail runs. Make sure your dog is in good physical condition and can handle the terrain.

Photography Adventures: Capture beautiful moments with your dog in picturesque settings. Explore parks, forests, and urban areas, and create a photo journal of your adventures.

Dog Sports: Consider getting involved in dog sports like agility, disc dog, or dock diving. These activities provide mental and physical challenges for your dog.

Exploring Urban Environments

In addition to outdoor adventures, urban environments offer ample opportunities for exploration. Discover dog-friendly urban spaces, visit dog parks, and take leisurely strolls through your city or town with your faithful companion by your side.

Before embarking on any adventure, ensure that your dog is well-trained, well-socialized, and in good health. Prioritize your dog's safety and comfort by packing necessary supplies, including water, food, first aid items, and any specific gear required for the activity. Always be sure to check local regulations and guidelines and be considerate of other people and wildlife when adventuring with your dog. The future for your well-trained and happy canine companion is bright, and together, you'll create a lifetime of cherished memories and experiences.

The Significance of Creating Lasting Memories with Your Canine Companion

Building lasting memories with your beloved canine is a heartwarming and rewarding experience that strengthens the bond between you and your four-legged friend. Dogs bring an abundance of joy, love, and companionship into our lives, and taking the time to create cherished moments together is essential. Here are some meaningful ways to forge enduring memories with your canine companion:

Quality Time: Spend quality time with your dog every day. Whether it's a cuddle on the couch, playtime in the backyard, or a leisurely walk, these daily interactions build a strong connection.

Training and Learning: Engage in positive reinforcement training sessions with your dog. Teaching new tricks, commands, and skills not only provides mental stimulation but also creates a sense of accomplishment for both you and your pup.

Adventure and Exploration: Venture out together on exciting adventures. Explore new hiking trails, visit dog-friendly beaches, and embark on road trips to discover new places.

Photography: Create a photo album or Instagram account dedicated to your dog's adventures. Capture candid moments, funny expressions, and milestones to cherish for years to come.

Celebrations: Mark special occasions in your dog's life, such as birthdays and adoption anniversaries, with dog-friendly cakes, parties, and memorable activities.

Vacations: Plan vacations that include your dog. Opt for pet-friendly accommodations and enjoy sightseeing, hiking, or relaxing with your furry friend by your side.

Dog Sports and Activities: Get involved in dog sports like agility, fly ball, or disc dog competitions. These activities not only provide exercise but also create a sense of achievement.

Volunteering: Consider volunteering together at animal shelters or visiting nursing homes as a therapy dog team. These experiences leave a positive impact on both your dog and the people you interact with.

Playdates: Arrange playdates with other dogs to allow your pup to socialize, play, and build friendships.

Special Outings: Treat your dog to special outings, such as visiting a dog-friendly restaurant or attending dog-related events in your community.

DIY Projects: Create DIY pet projects like homemade treats, toys, or a custom dog bed. Crafting together is a fun way to bond.

Training Adventures: Take your dog on training adventures to practice recall, obedience, and leash manners in different environments.

Spa Days: Pamper your dog with spa days, including grooming sessions, massages, and soothing baths.

Outdoor Movie Nights: Host outdoor movie nights in your backyard or at a pet-friendly venue, complete with comfy blankets and your dog's favorite snacks.

Camping Trips: Enjoy the great outdoors by going camping with your dog. Roast marshmallows by the campfire and stargaze together.

Holiday Traditions: Incorporate your dog into holiday traditions, such as dressing them up in costumes for Halloween or including them in holiday cards and decorations.

Quiet Moments: Sometimes, the most memorable moments are the quiet ones. Just sitting together and enjoying each other's company can create lasting memories.

Always prioritize your dog's comfort, safety, and well-being during all your activities. Your loyal canine companion will be with you through life's ups and downs. Tailor your adventures to suit your dog's personality and preferences, and savor every moment you share. Whether it's the ordinary routines or special occasions, each moment with your dog is an opportunity to craft treasured memories that will endure a lifetime.

The Importance of Advocacy for Positive Training

Promoting positive reinforcement training methods is not only advantageous for your dog but also fosters a more compassionate and humane approach to dog training. Advocacy for this training style is vital, and you can take several steps to advance this cause.

Advocacy for Positive Training

Your journey can inspire others to embrace positive reinforcement training methods. According to Friedman, (2010) it is important to remember to advocate for the welfare of dogs by promoting responsible ownership and positive training techniques because advocating for positive training with your dog is not only beneficial for your canine companion but also contributes to a more compassionate and humane approach to dog training overall.

Ways to Advocate for Positive Training

Educate Yourself: Start by educating yourself about positive training methods. Understand the principles behind positive reinforcement, operant conditioning, and how dogs learn. This knowledge will empower you to make informed choices in your dog's training.

Choose a Positive Trainer: When seeking professional training or guidance, select a certified positive reinforcement trainer or behaviorist. Look for credentials from reputable organizations like the Association of Professional Dog Trainers (APDT) or the International Association of Canine Professionals (IACP).

Share Your Positive Experiences: Share your success stories with positive training methods. Whether it's improved behavior, a stronger bond with your dog, or simply the joy of training together, share your positive experiences with others to inspire them to try positive training as well.

Be a Role Model: Demonstrate the effectiveness of positive training by showcasing your well-behaved and happy dog. When others see your dog's behavior and obedience, it can serve as a powerful example of positive training's benefits.

Advocate in Online Communities: Participate in online dog forums and social media groups to advocate for positive training. Share articles, videos, and resources that promote positive reinforcement techniques.

Organize Positive Training Events: Collaborate with local trainers or training organizations to host positive training workshops or seminars in your community. These events can educate dog owners and provide hands-on experience with positive methods.

Support Positive Training Legislation: Advocate for regulations and laws that promote the use of positive training methods and discourage the use of aversive techniques, such as shock collars or choke chains.

Challenge Misconceptions: When you encounter misconceptions or misunderstandings about positive training, respectfully share your knowledge and provide evidence of its effectiveness.

Promote Responsible Ownership: Emphasize the importance of responsible dog ownership, including proper socialization, training, and care. Encourage others to invest time and effort into training their dogs positively.

Be Patient and Compassionate: When discussing training methods with others, be patient and compassionate. Avoid confrontations and focus on providing information and resources to help them understand the benefits of positive training.

Share Resources: Share books, articles, and videos that promote positive training techniques with friends, family, and fellow dog owners.

Lead by Example: Set a positive example for others by always using positive reinforcement methods with your own dog, even in challenging situations.

Advocating for positive training methods not only benefits dogs but also contributes to a culture of kindness and empathy in the world of dog training. By sharing your knowledge and experiences, you can inspire others to adopt positive training techniques and provide a happier and healthier environment for their dogs.

Help Create a Bright Future for All Dogs

A brighter canine future is one where dogs are treated with love, respect, and empathy, and where their well-being is prioritized in every aspect of their lives. Achieving this brighter future for dogs involves various key elements:

Education: Educating dog owners and the general public about responsible pet ownership, positive training methods, and canine behavior is crucial. Knowledge empowers people to make informed decisions and provide the best care for their dogs.

Responsible Breeding: Promoting responsible breeding practices that prioritize the health and well-being of dogs over profit is essential. Reducing the prevalence of puppy mills and encouraging responsible breeding can lead to healthier canine generations.

Rescue and Adoption: Supporting rescue organizations and adopting dogs from shelters or rescues rather than purchasing from pet stores or online sellers helps reduce the number of homeless dogs. Adoption saves lives and provides loving homes for dogs in need.

Animal Welfare Legislation: Advocating for strong animal welfare laws and regulations ensures that dogs are protected from cruelty and neglect. Laws against animal cruelty, puppy mills, and inhumane training methods can create a safer environment for dogs.

Positive Training: Promoting positive reinforcement-based training methods fosters a culture of understanding and cooperation between dogs and their human companions. This approach leads to well-adjusted and obedient dogs without the need for punitive measures.

Healthcare Access: Ensuring that all dogs have access to quality healthcare, including vaccinations, preventive care, and veterinary treatment when needed, contributes to their overall well-being.

Behavioral Support: Providing resources for addressing behavioral issues in dogs, including anxiety and aggression, helps pet owners understand and manage these challenges effectively.

Socialization and Enrichment: Encouraging early socialization and providing mental and physical enrichment for dogs improves their behavior and mental health. Engaging in activities that stimulate their senses and provide mental challenges leads to happier, more content dogs.

Spaying and Neutering: Promoting spaying and neutering helps control the dog population and reduces the number of homeless dogs. It also offers health benefits to individual dogs.

Public Awareness Campaigns: Launching public awareness campaigns about responsible dog ownership, adoption, and the importance of treating dogs with kindness and respect can have a significant impact on canine well-being.

Compassion and Empathy: Fostering a culture of compassion and empathy toward dogs and all animals encourages individuals to treat them with the care and respect they deserve.

Community Support: Building supportive communities of dog owners, trainers, veterinarians, and rescue organizations creates a network of resources and expertise to help dogs and their owners thrive.

Research and Innovation: Continued research into canine behavior, health, and genetics can lead to improved understanding and innovative solutions to enhance the lives of dogs.

By collectively working toward these goals and advocating for the well-being of dogs, we can create a brighter future where dogs are cherished companions, treated with kindness, and enjoy happy, healthy lives as an integral part of our families and communities. With your commitment to positive training we continue to guide all dogs to a brighter future. We all play a part in creating a world where every dog thrives.

The Importance of Continuing Learning about Dogs and Positive Reinforcement Training

Continued learning about dogs is essential for responsible pet ownership and for fostering a deep, fulfilling bond with your canine companion. Dogs are complex and ever-evolving creatures, and staying informed about their behavior, health, and well-being is a rewarding endeavor.

Here are ways to continue learning about dogs:

Read Books: There is a wealth of literature on dog behavior, training, and care. Explore books by respected authors and experts in the field to deepen your understanding.

Online Courses: Many reputable organizations offer online courses on dog behavior, training, and health. These courses allow you to learn from experts and work at your own pace.

Attend Workshops and Seminars: Look for local or online workshops and seminars hosted by certified dog trainers, behaviorists, and veterinarians. These events often focus on specific topics and provide hands-on learning experiences.

Join Dog Clubs: Consider joining breed-specific clubs, agility groups, or other dog-related organizations in your community. These clubs often host events, share knowledge, and provide opportunities to learn from experienced dog owners.

Consult Professionals: If you encounter specific behavioral or health challenges with your dog, consult with veterinarians, certified trainers, or behaviorists. They can offer guidance and solutions tailored to your dog's needs.

Volunteer: Volunteering at animal shelters or rescue organizations can provide valuable insights into dog behavior and the challenges faced by homeless dogs. It's also a way to make a positive impact on the lives of dogs in need.

Follow Reputable Websites: Stay updated by following reputable websites and blogs dedicated to dog care, behavior, and training. Look for resources from veterinary clinics, universities, and respected dog organizations.

Participate in Dog Sports: Engage in dog sports like agility, obedience trials, or fly ball. These activities not only provide exercise but also offer a chance to learn from experienced trainers and handlers.

Attend Conferences: If you are passionate about dogs and have the opportunity, consider attending national or international dog-related conferences where you can learn from experts and network with other enthusiasts.

Engage in Citizen Science: Some organizations offer citizen science projects related to dog behavior and cognition. Participating can contribute to ongoing research and expand your knowledge.

Online Forums: Join online dog forums and communities to share experiences, ask questions, and learn from other dog owners. Be sure to choose reputable and moderated platforms.

Stay Inquisitive: Cultivate a curious mindset about dogs. Observe their behavior, ask questions, and seek answers to understand their needs and preferences better.

Learn About Breed Specifics: If you own a specific breed, take the time to learn about its unique characteristics, exercise requirements, and potential health concerns.

Continuously Train: Training is an ongoing process. Continue practicing commands, introducing new tricks, and reinforcing positive behavior throughout your dog's life.

Observe Your Dog: Pay attention to your dog's body language, vocalizations, and reactions in various situations. Understanding your dog's individual preferences and needs is invaluable.

Remember that every dog is unique, and what works for one may not work for another. Be open to adapting your approach based on your dog's personality and needs. Continue to learn, grow, and adapt your training methods as you and your dog face new challenges and opportunities [Arden and Adams, 2016]. Continued learning not only benefits your dog but also enhances the joy and fulfillment of your life together.

Final Thoughts for Your Successful Training Journey

As we conclude this exploration of the world of dog training, it is crucial to reflect on the shared success stories, the nurturing of a positive community of dog owners, and the promising future that awaits you and your well-trained, content canine companion.

Your commitment to positive reinforcement training and responsible pet ownership is not only transforming the lives of dogs but also strengthening the bond between humans and their furry companions. Together, we can create a world where every dog experiences love, happiness, and a fulfilling life.

As you continue on your journey, remember that it's not solely about training your dog; it's also about celebrating the journey itself, the shared experiences, and the countless joyful moments with your faithful companion.

Owning a dog is a cherished experience for millions of people worldwide. Dogs offer companionship, love, and loyalty, becoming cherished members of families. However, owning a dog comes with responsibilities, and proper training and care are essential for ensuring a harmonious relationship between humans and their canine companions.

According to Dunbar, (2012) positive reinforcement training is a methodology rooted in operant conditioning, a learning process where behavior is strengthened through the presentation of a desirable stimulus following the behavior in this training approach, desirable behaviors are rewarded, increasing the likelihood of their repetition. This stands in contrast to aversive methods that rely on punishment to discourage unwanted behaviors. Positive reinforcement training has gained popularity over the years, thanks to its numerous advantages and successes.

Positive reinforcement training is highly effective in facilitating a dog's learning and retention of desired behaviors. Dogs learn through trial and error, and when they receive rewards for performing desired actions, they are more likely to repeat those actions says Yin, (2015). Rooted in operant conditioning, this process strengthens the dog's comprehension of what is expected and encourages them to engage in appropriate behaviors.

According to Pryor (1999) positive reinforcement training fosters a strong bond between dogs and their owners. Dogs learn to trust their owners as this approach relies on rewards rather than punishment. This trust forms the foundation of a positive and co-operative relationship, allowing for effective communication and understanding between humans and dogs.

Another significant benefit of positive reinforcement training is its ability to reduce fear and aggression in dogs. By avoiding punitive measures, dogs are less likely to experience stress, anxiety, or fear during training (Blackwell et al., 2008). This approach helps prevent unwanted behaviors and aggression, creating a safer environment for both dogs and their human companions.

According to Arhant et al., (2010), positive reinforcement training is rooted in the neurobiology of reward systems. When a dog receives a reward for performing a desired behavior, it triggers the release of dopamine in their brain, creating a sense of pleasure and satisfaction. Positive reinforcement can stimulate the release of oxytocin, a hormone associated with bonding and social connection (Mendl et al., 2010). These neurobiological mechanisms contribute to the emotional well-being of dogs trained using positive reinforcement methods.

Furthermore, positive reinforcement training has a positive impact on a dog's emotional well-being. Dogs trained through positive reinforcement are less likely to experience anxiety, fear, or stress during training sessions (Horowitz, 2009). They associate training with positive experiences, creating a sense of happiness and contentment.

Ethical considerations in dog training are closely tied to the choice of training methods. Positive reinforcement training aligns with ethical principles, emphasizing the well-being and humane treatment of dogs.

A primary ethical concern in dog training revolves around the well-being of the animals. As highlighted by Hiby et al. (2004), positive reinforcement training places a high priority on preventing pain and distress in dogs. This approach, developed and refined over the past eight decades, emphasizes the use of rewards while avoiding the infliction of pain or distress. The significant success of positive reinforcement training has made it one of the most frequently endorsed and employed training styles. Consequently, it underscores the imperative that training must never jeopardize a dog's physical or emotional health, embodying a fundamental principle of ethical training.

Dog owners and trainers have ethical responsibilities to ensure the well-being of the animals in their care. Promoting the dog's well-being should always be the primary goal (Yin, 2015). This includes using training methods based on positive reinforcement, creating a safe and stimulating environment, and meeting the dog's physical and emotional needs.

Positive reinforcement training is a versatile and effective approach that can be applied to various aspects of dog training. Two fundamental techniques in positive reinforcement training are clicker training and treat-based training. Clicker training involves using a small device that makes a clicking sound to signal when the dog has performed a desired behavior correctly. Treat-based training, as the name suggests, relies on the use of food rewards to reinforce positive behaviors (Dunbar, 2012).

Positive reinforcement training can effectively address common behavioral issues in dogs. For example, housebreaking, a challenging aspect of puppy training, can be facilitated through positive reinforcement techniques (Yin, 2015). Similarly, aggression issues can be managed and mitigated using positive reinforcement methods (Blackwell et al., 2008).

Positive reinforcement training is not limited to basic obedience. It can also be applied to train dogs for specific purposes, such as service dogs and therapy dogs. These dogs need specialized training to perform their tasks effectively, and positive reinforcement methods provide a humane and successful approach to achieving these goals (Pryor, 1999).

While positive reinforcement training offers numerous benefits, it is not without its challenges and criticisms.

One of the primary challenges in positive reinforcement training is the need for consistency and patience. Training dogs using positive reinforcement requires time and effort, and it may take longer to see results compared to aversive methods (Yin, 2015). Dog owners and trainers must remain patient and consistent in their approach.

According to Arhant et al., (2010) dogs are individuals, and their responses to training may vary. Some dogs may be more responsive to positive reinforcement, while others may require different approaches. Understanding and adapting to individual dog characteristics is essential for successful positive reinforcement training.

Positive reinforcement training sometimes faces criticism due to misconceptions and myths. Some people believe that it involves permissiveness or that it is less effective than aversive methods (Hiby et al., 2004). These misconceptions can hinder the widespread adoption of positive reinforcement training.

Training dogs for complex behaviors or tasks may require additional considerations and specialized techniques. While positive reinforcement can be effective in many situations, complex behaviors may require a combination of methods or more advanced training approaches (Pryor, 1999).

Scientific research provides strong support for the effectiveness of positive reinforcement training methods.

Studies have consistently shown that positive reinforcement is an effective way to train dogs. For example, a study by Blackwell et al. (2008) found that training methods based on positive reinforcement were associated with fewer behavior problems reported by owners. Another study by Arhant et al. (2010) demonstrated that positive reinforcement training methods were effective for both smaller and larger dogs, emphasizing its versatility.

Furthermore, cognitive and behavioral science research has contributed to the understanding of why positive reinforcement is so effective. The release of dopamine and oxytocin during training sessions has been demonstrated through neurobiological research (Mendl et al., 2010). This evidence supports the claim that positive reinforcement leads to increased emotional well-being in dogs.

Alongside effective training methods, responsible dog ownership is crucial to ensuring the well-being of dogs and the harmony of their coexistence with humans.

Responsible dog ownership begins with providing proper nutrition and healthcare. Dogs require a balanced diet, regular exercise, and access to clean water (Dunbar, 2012). Routine veterinary care, including vaccinations and preventive measures, is essential for maintaining a dog's health.

Dogs are intelligent and active animals that need mental and physical stimulation to stay happy and healthy. Owners should engage their dogs in stimulating activities, such as interactive toys, puzzle games, and daily walks (Pryor, 1999).

A responsible dog owner ensures that their dog has a safe and stimulating environment. This includes securing the home and yard to prevent accidents or escapes (Yin, 2015). Providing appropriate toys and activities within the living space keeps the dog mentally engaged.

Proper socialization is vital for dogs to become well-adjusted and confident members of society. Socialization should begin early in a dog's life to ensure they are comfortable around people, other dogs, and various environments (Blackwell et al., 2008). In addition to socialization, ongoing training helps dogs develop good manners and appropriate behavior in various situations.

Responsible dog ownership benefits not only the dogs themselves but also the community and the owners.

Responsible dog owners contribute to safer and more harmonious communities. Well-trained and well-behaved dogs are less likely to cause disruptions or pose risks to neighbors, pedestrians, or other animals (Hiby et al., 2004). This fosters a positive environment for all.

Owning a dog has been associated with numerous health benefits for humans. Regular exercise with a dog can improve cardiovascular health, reduce stress, and increase overall physical activity levels (Dunbar, 2012). The emotional support and companionship provided by dogs have positive effects on mental well-being.

The emotional and psychological well-being of dog owners is often greatly enhanced by their furry companions. The bond formed between a dog and its owner can provide comfort, reduce feelings of loneliness, and boost overall happiness (Pryor, 1999).

Positive reinforcement training is a humane and effective approach to training dogs, offering numerous benefits such as enhanced learning, a strengthened bond, and reduced fear and aggression. It aligns with ethical principles, emphasizing the well-being of dogs and promoting responsible dog ownership. Responsible dog ownership includes providing proper care, mental and physical stimulation, a safe environment, and socialization. These responsibilities not only benefit the dogs themselves but also contribute to healthier communities and improved well-being for dog owners. Therefore, the enduring importance of positive reinforcement training and encouragement for responsible dog ownership cannot be understated. By following these principles, dog owners can ensure a happy, healthy, and harmonious relationship with their canine companions.

REFERENCES

American Veterinary Society of Animal Behavior. (2008).

Position Statement on Puppy Socialization. Retrieved from https://avsab.org/wp-content/uploads/2019/01/Puppy-Socialization-Position-Statement-FINAL.pdf

Appleby, D. L., Bradshaw, J. W. S., & Casey, R. A. (2002). Relationships between aggressive and avoidance behavior by dogs and their experience in the first six months of life. The Veterinary Record, 150(17), 511-514.

Arden, C., & Adams, M. J. (2016). Handbook of Applied Dog Behavior and Training, Volume Two: Etiology and Assessment of Behavior Problems. John Wiley & Sons.

Arhant, C., Bubna-Littitz, H., Bartels, A., Futschik, A., & Troxler, J. (2010). Behavior of smaller and larger dogs: Effects of training methods, inconsistency of owner behavior and level of engagement in activities with the dog. Applied Animal Behavior Science, 123(3-4), 131-142.

Bailey, J., & Burch, M. R. (1999). How dogs learn. Howell Book House.

Blackwell, E. J., Twells, C., Seawright, A., & Casey, R. A. (2008). The relationship between training methods and the occurrence of behavior problems, as reported by owners, in a population of domestic dogs. Journal of Veterinary Behavior: Clinical Applications and Research, 3(5), 207-217.

Borchelt, P. L., & Voith, V. L. (1982). Dominance aggression in dogs: Description, interpretation, and treatment. Journal of the American Veterinary Medical Association, 180(7), 769-775.

Donaldson, J. (2008). Culture clash: A revolutionary new way of understanding the relationship between humans and domestic dogs. James & Kenneth Publishers.

Deldalle, S., & Gaunet, F. (2014). Effects of 2 training methods on stress-related behaviors of the dog (Canis familiaris) and on the dog–owner relationship. Journal of Veterinary Behavior, 9(2), 58-65.

Dunbar, I. S. (1996). Dog behavior and training: Veterinary advice for owners. Howell Book House.

Dunbar, I. S. (2012). Before and after getting your puppy: The positive approach to raising a happy, healthy, and well-behaved dog. New World Library.

Fox, M. W. (1978). The critical period for socialization of puppies. Journal of Veterinary Medical Education, 162(12), 1164-1166.

Freedman, D. G., King, J. A., & Elliot, O. (1961). Critical Period in the Social Development of Dogs. Science, 133(3457), 1016-1017.

Friedman, S. G. (2010). What's wrong with this picture? Effectiveness is not enough. Journal of Applied Companion Animal Behavior, 4(1), 48-51.

Fry, D. B., & Patronek, G. J. (2014). Comparative welfare of crated and uncrated dogs housed in a laboratory. Journal of Applied Animal Welfare Science, 17(3), 236-246.

Gazzano, A., Zilocchi, M., Massoni, E., & Mariti, C. (2010). Dogs' coping styles and dog-handler relationships influence avalanche search team performance. Applied Animal Behavior Science, 123(3-4), 131-142.

Herron, M. E., Shofer, F. S., & Reisner, I. R. (2009). Survey of the use and outcome of confrontational and non-confrontational training methods in client-owned dogs showing undesired behaviors. Applied Animal Behavior Science, 117(1-2), 47-54.

Hiby, E. F., Rooney, N. J., & Bradshaw, J. W. S. (2004). Dog training methods: Their use, effectiveness and interaction with behavior and welfare. Animal Welfare, 13(1), 63-69.

Horowitz, I. (2009). Inside of a dog: What dogs see, smell, and know. Simon and Schuster.

Horowitz, A. (2009). Disambiguating the "guilty look": Salient prompts to a familiar dog behavior. Behavioral Processes, 81(3), 447-452.

Landsberg, G. M., Hunthausen, W. L., & Ackerman, L. (2013). Behavior problems of the dog and cat. Elsevier Health Sciences.

Lit, L., Schweitzer, J. B., & Oberbauer, A. M. (2010). Handler beliefs affect scent detection dog outcomes. Animal Cognition, 13(3), 379-388.

Mendl, M., Brooks, J., Basse, C., Burman, O., Paul, E., & Blackwell, E. (2010). Dogs showing separation-related behavior exhibit a 'pessimistic' cognitive bias. Current Biology, 20(19), R839-R840.

McConnell, P. B. (2002). The Other End of the Leash: Why We Do What We Do Around Dogs. Random House.

Overall, K. (2013). Manual of Clinical Behavioral Medicine for Dogs and Cats. Elsevier Health Sciences.

Pryor, K. (1999). Don't shoot the dog! The new art of teaching and training. Bantam.

Reid, P. (1996). Excel-erated Learning: Explaining in Plain English How Dogs Learn and How Best to Teach Them. James & Kenneth Publishers.

Rooney, N. J., & Cowan, S. (2011). Training methods and owner–dog interactions: Links with dog behavior and learning ability. Applied Animal Behavior Science, 132(3-4), 169-177.

Scott, J. P., & Fuller, J. L. (1965). Genetics and the Social Behavior of the Dog. University of Chicago Press.

Serpell, J. A. (1996). Influence of breed on the occurrence of behavior problems in dogs. Applied Animal Behavior Science, 47(1-2), 1-8.

Thompson, K., mith, B. P., & Deakin, A. (2017). Behavioral and physiological responses of dogs to immersion in water: An exploratory study. Veterinary Medicine: Research and Reports, 8, 35-43.

Turid Rugaas. (2005). On Talking Terms with Dogs: Calming Signals. Dogwise Publishing.

Landsberg, G. M., Melese, P., Sherman, B. L., & Neilson, J. C. (2008). Effectiveness of fluoxetine chewable tablets in the treatment of canine separation anxiety. Journal of Veterinary Behavior: Clinical Applications and Research, 3(1), 12-19.

McGowan, R. T., Bolte, C., Barnett, H. R., & Perez-Camargo, G. (2013). Behavioral and physiological responses of dogs entering rehoming kennels. Physiology & Behavior, 12(0), 101-106.

Miller, S. C., & Luescher, A. U. (2017). The Manual of Clinical Behavioral Medicine for Dogs and Cats. Elsevier Health Sciences.

O'Farrell, V., & Bath, A. (2008). Behavioral problems in dogs with aggression against people. Part 2: Clinical diagnosis and treatment. In Pract, 30(6), 284-290.

Pryor, K. (2009). Clicker training for dogs. Simon and Schuster.

Salman, M. D., Hutchison, J., Ruch-Gallie, R., Kogan, L., New Jr, J. C.,

Kass, P. H., & Scarlett, J. M. (2000). Behavioral reasons for relinquishment of dogs and cats to 12 shelters. Journal of Applied Animal Welfare Science, 3(2), 93-106.

Salvin, H. E., McGreevy, P. D., Sachdev, P. S., & Valenzuela, M. J. (2011). The effect of breed on age-related changes in behavior and disease prevalence in cognitively normal older community dogs (Canis lupus familiaris). Journal of Veterinary Behavior, 6(4), 339-345.

Scott, J. P., & Fuller, J. L. (1965). Genetics and the Social Behavior of the Dog. University of Chicago Press.

Teng, K. T., McGreevy, P. D., Toribio, J. A., Dhand, N. K., & Ankeny, D. P. (2010). Effects of castration on problem behaviors in male dogs with reference to age and duration of behavior. Journal of Veterinary Behavior, 5(8), 11-17.

Wan, M., Bolger, N., & Champagne, F. A. (2008). Human perception of fear in dogs varies according to experience with dogs. PLoS ONE, 3(12), e3847.

Yin, S. (2015). How to behave so your dog behaves. TFH Publications.

Canine Behavior Modification Plan

Trainer Name:	Date:
Location:	Phone:

Dog Name:

Breed:

Age:

Owners Name:

Owners Address:

Emergency Contact:

Phone:

Behavior Issue:

Comments:

Required Modification:

<table>
<tr><td>Action Plan:

Due Date:</td></tr>
</table>

Guardian's Signature: _____________________________ Date: _____________

Trainers Signature: _____________________________ Date: _____________

Follow-up:

Date:	Comment:	Trainer Initials:
Date:	Comment:	Trainer Initials:

Appendix A: Canine Behavior Modification Plan

Canine Behavior Modification Plan

Trainer Name:	Date:
Location:	Phone:

Dog Name:
Breed:
Age:
Owners Name:
Owners Address:

Emergency Contact:
Phone:

Behavior Issue:

Comments:

Required Modification:

Action Plan:
Due Date:

Guardian's Signature: _________________________ Date: _____________

Trainers Signature: _________________________ Date: _____________

Follow-up:

Date:	Comment:	Trainer Initials:
Date:	Comment:	Trainer Initials:

Appendix B: Canine Training Schedule

Canine Training Schedule

Training Schedule	Date	Day	Day	Day	Day	Day
Handler:						
Command:						
Technique:						
# of Sessions:						
# of Repetitions:						
Length of Sessions:						
Motivation(1-5):						
# of Places (1-20):						
# of People (1-20):						
Accuracy %:						
Distraction Level (1-5):						
Percentage of Completion:						
Reinforcement Schedule 100-5%:						

Notes:

Appendix B: Canine Training Schedule

Canine Training Schedule

Training Schedule	Date	Day	Day	Day	Day	Day
Handler:						
Command:						
Technique:						
# of Sessions:						
# of Repetitions:						
Length of Sessions:						
Motivation(1-5):						
# of Places (1-20):						
# of People (1-20):						
Accuracy %:						
Distraction Level (1-5):						
Percentage of Completion:						
Reinforcement Schedule 100-5%:						

Notes:

Dog Training Mini-Session

Date:	Time:

Location:
Behavior:
Reps:
Successful:
If you rated 80% or greater, it is time to increase the criteria.
Notes:

Date:	Time:

Location:
Behavior:
Reps:
Successful:
If you rated 80% or greater, it is time to increase the criteria.
Notes:

Date:	Time:

Location:
Behavior:
Reps:
Successful:
If you rated 80% or greater, it is time to increase the criteria.
Notes:

Appendix C: Dog Training Mini-Session

Dog Training Mini-Session

Date:	Time:

Location:
Behavior:
Reps:
Successful:
If you rated 80% or greater, it is time to increase the criteria.
Notes:

Date:	Time:

Location:
Behavior:
Reps:
Successful:
If you rated 80% or greater, it is time to increase the criteria.
Notes:

Date:	Time:

Location:	
Behavior:	
# Reps:	
# Successful:	
If you rated 80% or greater, it is time to increase the criteria.	
Notes:	

Appendix D: General Dog Command Assessment

General Dog Command Assessment

Dog Name: ____

	Poor	Okay	Good	Great	Perfect
Sit	○	○	○	○	○
Stay	○	○	○	○	○
On	○	○	○	○	○
Off	○	○	○	○	○
Touch	○	○	○	○	○
Roll Over	○	○	○	○	○
Leave It	○	○	○	○	○
Focus	○	○	○	○	○
Come	○	○	○	○	○
Heel	○	○	○	○	○
Drop it	○	○	○	○	○
Paw	○	○	○	○	○
Sit Pretty	○	○	○	○	○
Jump	○	○	○	○	○

Appendix D: General Dog Command Assessment

General Dog Command Assessment

Dog Name: ____

	Poor	Okay	Good	Great	Perfect
_____________	○	○	○	○	○
_____________	○	○	○	○	○
_____________	○	○	○	○	○
_____________	○	○	○	○	○
_____________	○	○	○	○	○
_____________	○	○	○	○	○
_____________	○	○	○	○	○
_____________	○	○	○	○	○
_____________	○	○	○	○	○
_____________	○	○	○	○	○
_____________	○	○	○	○	○
_____________	○	○	○	○	○
_____________	○	○	○	○	○
_____________	○	○	○	○	○

Appendix E: Service Dog Command Assessment

Service Dog Command Assessment

Dog Name: ____

	Poor	Okay	Good	Great	Perfect
No	○	○	○	○	○
Block	○	○	○	○	○
Under	○	○	○	○	○
Peak	○	○	○	○	○
Back	○	○	○	○	○
Wait	○	○	○	○	○
Stand	○	○	○	○	○
Focus	○	○	○	○	○
Place	○	○	○	○	○
Let's Go	○	○	○	○	○
Drop it	○	○	○	○	○
Paw	○	○	○	○	○
Sit Pretty	○	○	○	○	○
Jump	○	○	○	○	○

Appendix E: Service Dog Command Assessment

Service Dog Command Assessment

Dog Name: ____

	Poor	Okay	Good	Great	Perfect
_______________	○	○	○	○	○
_______________	○	○	○	○	○
_______________	○	○	○	○	○
_______________	○	○	○	○	○
_______________	○	○	○	○	○
_______________	○	○	○	○	○
_______________	○	○	○	○	○
_______________	○	○	○	○	○
_______________	○	○	○	○	○
_______________	○	○	○	○	○
_______________	○	○	○	○	○
_______________	○	○	○	○	○
_______________	○	○	○	○	○
_______________	○	○	○	○	○

Appendix F: Canine Socialization Checklist

Canine Socialization Checklist

Dog Name: ____

People

☐ Adults	☐ Different Ethnicities	☐ Bike Riders	☐ People with Sunglasses
☐ Toddlers	☐ People with Disabilities	☐ Crowds	☐ People with Dark Clothing
☐ Children	☐ Joggers	☐ Mailman	☐ People with Hats
☐ Seniors	☐ Skateboarders	☐ People in Uniform	☐ Other

Being Touched or Handled

☐ Brushing	☐ Teeth brushed	☐ Being picked up	☐ Groomed with grooming shears
☐ Trimming Nails	☐ Tail lifted	☐ Being hugged	☐ Groomed with electric clippers
☐ Dried with a Towel	☐ Touch and move testicles	☐ Being carried	☐ Blow dryer
☐ Bathed	☐ Lift Tail	☐ Being laid on	☐
☐ Touch Ears	☐ Wearing a Harness	☐ Sitting on a lap	☐
☐ Cleaning Ears and Removing ear hair if needed	☐ Wearing a collar	☐ Pet by children	☐
☐ Paws touched	☐ Leash Walking	☐ Belly scratches	☐

Places

☐ Veterinarian Office	☐ Park	☐ School	☐ Puppy Classes
☐ Groomer	☐ Lake	☐ Hospital	☐ Staircases
☐ Car Ride	☐ Elevator	☐ City/Town	☐ Bridges
☐ Home Depot	☐ Escalator	☐ Shopping Area	☐ Nighttime
☐ Library	☐ Waterpark	☐ Firework Show	☐ Other

Appendix F: Canine Socialization Checklist

Canine Socialization Checklist

Continued

Sounds

☐ Sirens	☐ Motorcycle	☐ Doorbell	☐ Vacuum Cleaner
☐ Train horn	☐ Fireworks	☐ Music	☐ Lawnmower
☐ Band/Football Game	☐ Tractors	☐ Barking Dogs	☐ Gunshots
☐ Cars	☐ Television	☐ Dishwasher	☐ Thunder
☐ Alarm Clock	☐ Children Playing loudly	☐ Sound Machine	☐ Other

Surfaces

☐ Pavement	☐ Grass	☐ Slick floors	☐ Sand
☐ Rocks	☐ Wood chips	☐ Hardwood Floors	☐ Carpet
☐ Asphalt	☐ Rubber mulch	☐ Cement Floor	☐ Water/puddles
☐ Leaves	☐ Snow/Ice	☐ Bricks	☐ Mud
☐ Tile/Stone Floor	☐ Linoleum Floors	☐ Reflective Surfaces	☐ Other

Animals

☐ Puppies	☐ Different temperaments	☐ Cats	☐ Rabbits
☐ Older dogs	☐ Flat faced dogs	☐ Horses	☐ Birds
☐ Different breeds	☐ Farm Animals	☐ Squirrels/ chipmunks	☐ Ducks/Geese
☐ Cows	☐ Reptiles	☐ Guinea Pigs/ hamsters, mice	☐ Other

Objects

☐ Fans	☐ Brooms	☐ Balloons	☐ Clothing
☐ Bags	☐ Umbrella	☐ Skateboards	☐ Wheel Chairs
☐ Shopping Cart	☐ Paper	☐ Trash Cans	☐ Walker
☐ Shovels	☐ Pots and Pans	☐ Agility Obstacles	☐ Squeakers
☐ Toys	☐ Bed	☐ Sofa/Couch	☐ Other

Index

Behavior Challenge Prevention

Behavior Challenge Resolution

Behavior Challenges

ABOUT THE AUTHOR

Kristin Leest, a native of Newtown, Connecticut, developed a deep-seated affection for animals during her upbringing. This passion was something she shared with her grandmother, who dedicated over three decades to running an animal welfare organization. This early influence played a significant role in nurturing her love and enthusiasm for poodles, a passion that remained with her over the years.

In 2009, Kristin took a significant step by becoming a certified dog trainer, embarking on a journey to work closely with dogs. In 2012, with the arrival of her first son, it became clear that adding a poodle to the family was a top priority.

Today, Kristin resides in Charleston, South Carolina, with her husband Martin, her son, Ryan, her three stepchildren, Maggie, Walter, and Patrick and her totally awesome poodle crew of seven! (Heidi, Riley, Roxy, Ruby, Ginger, Nala and Hank) Kristin's venture, "Simply Standard Poodles," focuses on raising and breeding fully health tested American Kennel Club standard poodles for family pets, service dogs and agility competition canines. Additionally, she operates a dog health and Wellness Company, "Pawsitivity," dedicated to providing natural supplements, vitamins, and all the essential elements required for dogs to lead their best lives, fostering a spirit of Pawsitivity. A portion of all the sales at Pawsitivity go to local animal rescues and animal shelters to support the entire canine communities' wellness initiative.

Visit Kristin at:

www.caninepawsitivity.com